CHILE: An Anthology of New Writing

CHILE:

An Anthology of New Writing

Selected and Edited by
Miller Williams

The Kent State University Press

ACKNOWLEDGMENTS

Poems by Miguel Arteche appeared in *Destierro y Tinieblas* (Zig-Zag, Stgo., 1963 ©). Efraín Barquero: "Te Andan Sueños" and "Mi Amada Esta Tejiendo" appeared in *La Compañera* (Nascimento, Stgo., 1956 ©), and "La Miel Heredada" appeared in his book *Enjambre*. The poems by Rolando Cárdenas appeared in *El Invierno de la Provincia* (Sociedad de Escritores de Chile, Editorial Universitaria, Stgo., © R. C. 1963). "El Final" by Poli Délano appeared in *Gente Solitaria* (Ediciones Mazorca, Imprenta Alfa, Stgo., 1960 ©). The poems by Luisa Johnson appeared in *Horario de un Caracol* (Armando Mendin, Stgo., 1964 ©). The poems of Enrique Lihn appeared in *La Pieza Oscura* (Editorial Universitaria, Stgo., © E. L. 1963). The poems by Nicanor Parra are from *Versos de Salón* (Nascimento, Stgo., 1962 ©). The poems of Alberto Rubio appeared in *La Greda Vasija* (Stgo., 1952 © A. R.). "First Comes The Sea" by Antonio Skarmeta appeared in *El Boletín del Instituto Nacional de Chile*. "Fin del Mundo" and "To A Boy in A Tree" by Jorge Teillier appeared in *Poemas del Pais de Nunca Jamás* (Menedin, Stgo., 1963 ©); the other poems by Sr. Teillier are from *El Árbol de la Memoria* (Imprenta Alfa, Stgo., 1960 ©). The poems of Armando Uribe Arce: "La Lengua Habla" and "No Se Mi Nombre" appeared in his book *Los Obstáculos*, Colección Adonis (Madrid, 1961); "Quien Eres Tu," "Yo Te Amo" and "Es Como Una Enfermedad" appeared in *El Engañoso Laúd* (Ediciones del Joven Laurel, Editorial Universitaria, Stgo., 1956 ©). Some of the poems by Barquero, Parra, Rubio, and Teillier have appeared in *Chicago Review*; by Arteche, Barquero, Lihn, Parra, Teillier, and Uribe in *Motive*; by Arteche, Barquero, Lihn, and Teillier in *Prairie Schooner*; the interview the Nicanor Parra is reprinted from *Shenandoah*, The Washington and Lee University Review, Volume 18, Number 1, by permission of the editor. The poems by Pablo Neruda are reprinted by permission of the author and appeared in *Estravagria* (Editorial Lozada, Buenos Aires, 1958 ©).

CONTENTS

Illustrations:
Nemesio Antunez
Cecilia Bruna

INTRODUCTION

ELIOT freed a generation of writers from the old chains of theme and form, and shackled them in newly forged links of something called style, while Thomas and Cummings were not quite able to free us from anything, precisely because we were unable to take their lines, their looks, as ours — they were too eccentrically their own. The liberator is always the new ruler. So Pablo Neruda, releasing the poets of Chile from the bonds of precedence, the overbearing omnipresence of the accepted poetry — most of which might have been produced by the Spanish Academy itself — imposed, whether he would have had it so or not, the style of his own writing, his own theme and form, and the color of his own thoughts on a whole generation of poets. When a man can't free himself, he follows whoever can. So Neruda, for a long time, was the great influence.

He made the language do things it hadn't done before. He gave it a terseness and a flexibility it hadn't known. He made the gerund do tricks. He revamped the grammar. He was, as every great writer finally has to be, his own academy. And for a generation, young poets were writing bad Neruda, as we were writing bad Eliot and bad Auden.

But the influence of a man is not as durable as the influence of a century, and it diminishes less dramatically. The younger poets of Chile are leaving Neruda at last to his own greatness, are stepping out of the shadow of that greatness, and are beginning to look about themselves at their own lives, to react with their own senses, in their own voices. Nicanor Parra with his "antipoems"; Enrique Lihn with his dark, introspective lyrics; Armando Uribe with his short verses that call to mind Pound, the *Rubaiyat*, and haiku — these and others are building a new body of poetry in Chile, where, as in the English-speaking countries, it is a time not of revolution but of consolidation.

And this sort of age can be an age of tension. There are those who would like to go on to a new language, new forms, to experiment and expand, and there are those who want to keep the links between the generations joined in a surer way than they sometimes seem to be. This conflict exists not only between poets, but within poets, so that in a single poem, contemporary in its overall tone, modern in most of its language and attitudes, we find haunting the lines like ghosts from the past, mysterious moonlight and graveyards of ships and an incredible number of nightingales. The poetry of Chile is a poetry with a great history, enriched by that history and now pulling as free of it as a poetry ever can or should pull free, moving at random, speaking with many voices, hunting itself, experimenting, changing.

The prose is less "Chilean," as Chile holds its prose by a thinner history. This is not to say that the stories here could have come from any place. Most works that could have been done in any country, any time, are not worth printing. These could have come only from South America — if not only from Chile — only now. But as the gifts of the past to the prose writers of today are smaller than those the poets are heir to, so are the chains of influence lighter. The prose is more freewheeling, more relaxed than much of the poetry.

Let me say, though, that neither in the case of poetry nor fiction has there been an attempt to include only the best of the best known; here is a wide spectrum of ideas and styles, something of what Chile is.

Any view of Chile which doesn't include Neruda, of course, would be a false view. He is, and he will continue to be, a great presence. He has given us six poems which are translated into English here for the first time.

There are many things about Chile's writers which don't show up in the poems and the stories — Parra's rustic cabin at the foothills of the mountains, where you arrive winded and welcome; the Latin dance called talking; the endless political theorizing — and everything happens over good Chilean wine in the blue shadow of the Andes. It happens continually, all day and all night. The purpose of this issue is to catch some of it happening.

This is as good a time as any to thank the executors of the Amy Lowell Traveling Scholarship in Poetry, under which grant for 1963-64 I went to Chile and began collecting material, and the Louisiana State University Research Council, whose very generous grants supplemented the scholarship.

A special long-distance thanks to those who were kind enough to help with the translating, to Poli Delano, who put me in touch with many writers, to Luisa Johnson, who made possible a rewarding meeting with Pablo Neruda and who helped me make contact with several artists, to Nicanor Parra, for giving his time and thought to the interview, and to all those writers and artists who helped introduce me to Chile, entertained me in their homes, and showed me the streets to see.

Some of those streets are here.

MILLER WILLIAMS
New Orleans, Louisiana
1967

OPPOSITE

Nemesio Antunez (1918) studied architecture, but never practiced it. He lived for ten years in Europe and the United States, returning to Chile in 1953. He is the founder of the famous *Taller 99*, a workshop of the art of engraving. In 1958 he was awarded the Wolf Prize as the best painter in Latin America. His one-man shows have been held in Washington, New York, Paris, Oslo, Buenos Aires, Sao Paulo, Rio de Janeiro, Lima, and Santiago. Since 1962 he has been Director of the Museum of Contemporary Art of the University of Chile.

MIGUEL ARTECHE

Translated by
MILLER WILLIAMS

Miguel Arteche, born in 1926, is the author of nine books of poems which have brought him a number of awards, including one in the Concurso Gabriela Mistral de Poesia in 1958. In 1964 he was chosen to the Chilean Academy of Language. A devout Roman Catholic in a country where writers generally share the anti-clerical feeling of the great majority of the people, Arteche's work is fully dedicated to his faith. He is now Cultural Attaché with the Chilean Embassy in Madrid.

EPITALAMIO

Ganamos en las horas de la carne,
pero perdimos, luego, la batalla,
cuando luchando a solas en las plumas
de la noche doblamos la cabeza.
El mar rodeó la sábana mortuoria
de Venus, sin espuma:

y bogando volamos los planetas
de aquella madrugada que surgia
gemela entre tus pechos temblorosos.
Perdimos en los siglos de la carne;
pero ganamos, luego, la derrota
cuando luchando a ciegas en las brumas
del amor libertamos nuestro abrazo.

EPITHALAMIUM

We win in the hour of the flesh
but we lose, later, the battle,
when fighting alone in the feathers
of the night we turn our heads.
The sea surrounded the funeral sheet
of Venus without foam:

and rocking we flung the planets away
from the dawn that rose
twin in your trembling breasts.
We lose in the centuries of the flesh:
but we win, later, the defeat
when fighting blind in the haze
of love we let go our embrace.

GIRANDO

Y ahora en el espacio, en el oscuro espacio
de la estrella, en una habitación que desconozco:
en el espacio
sin campo,
sin lluvia,
sin manos
y sin ciudades. Ahora: en el espacio,
donde no habita nadie, donde la oscuridad es llanto
sin respuesta. Solo, con una silla, y desnudo,
canto:
pero no tengo voz, pero no tengo manos.
Gira y arde en el espacio
mi habitación desnuda. Y canto
a ver si me responden desde abajo.

Y veo cómo se rompen las paredes,
y veo la luz, y clamo
por las palabras que no brotan. Y el resplandor se acerca
girando.
Pero no es tu luz, Dios mío, y el espacio
salta en la noche perdurable. Y vuelvo
a cantar,
por ver si me responden desde abajo.

GOLF

El gallo trae la espina.
La espina trae el ladrón.
El ladrón la bofetada.
Hora de sexta en el sol.

SPINNING

And now in space, in the dark space
of the stars, in a habitation I don't know:
in space
without field,
without rain,
without hands
and without cities. Now: in space
where no one is, where darkness is a sad cry
with no answer. Alone, with a chair, and naked,
I sing:
But I have no voice, but I have no hands.
My naked habitation spins and blazes in space.
I sing
to see if there is an answer from below.

And I see how the walls are broken,
and I see the light, and I shout
with words that never break through. And the splendor comes
closer spinning.
But it is not your light, my God, and space
leaps in the everlasting night. And I turn
to sing,
to see if there is an answer from below.

GOLF

The rooster brings the thorn.
The thorn brings the thief.
The thief brings the blow.
In the sixth hour of the sun.

Y el caballero hipnotiza
una pelota de golf.

Tiembla el huerto con la espada.
A sangre tienen sabor
las aguas que da el olivo.
El gallo otra vez cantó.

Y el caballero golpea
una pelota de golf.

Traen túnica de grana.
Visten de azote al perdón.
Y el salivazo correo
del uno al tres del amor.

Y el caballero que corre
tras la pelota de golf.

Duda el clavo y el vinagre,
y duda el procurador,
y a las tinieblas se llevan
huesos desiertos de Dios.

Y el caballero recoge
una pelota de golf.

Negro volumen de hieles.
La lluvia del estertor.
Ojos vacíos de esponja
negra para su voz.
Relámpago que el costado
penetró.
Cordillera del martillo
que clavó.
Vestiduras divididas
por el puño del tembler.

Se arrodilló el caballero
por su pelota de golf.

And the gentleman hypnotizes
a golf ball.

The garden trembles with the sword.
The water of olives
has the taste of blood.
Again the rooster sang.

And the gentleman hits
a golf ball.

They bring a robe of scarlet.
They dress forgiveness in lashes.
And the saliva corrodes
the one into three of love.

And the gentleman runs after
a golf ball.

The nail and the vinegar doubt,
the solicitor doubts.
They bear to the darkness
the deserted bones of God.

And the gentleman finds
the golf ball.

Black volumes of bile.
Death-rattle rain.
Empty eyes of a black sponge
for his voice.
Lightning tearing into his side.
From the hammering mallet, mountains.
Vestments ripped by the fist
of the earthquake.

The gentleman kneels
beside the golf ball.

ELEGIA POR UN NIÑO MUERTO

Y el niño abrió los ojos en la noche, y las plumas
   de la muerte rozaron su corazón: la fiebre
      cantó sobre los hilos de las venas.
Y vi los corrosivos dedos sobre su boca,
y el serpentino tajo que segaba implacable
      todo el tallo del pulso.

          Entonces,
   cuando en el cielo el viento se acercaba,
          ¡ay sólo entonces!,
          rogué a solas por él.

Y el niño ardió en la noche, y las cárdenas uñas
se hundieron en la tierna yema: sobre sus ojos
      cintilaron las últimas estrellas.
Y vi los dientes nítricos royendo el virgen tuétano,
   y en el centro del pecho desmoronado todas
      las hojas de su sangre.

          Entonces,
   cuando en la sombra el trueno penetraba,
          ¡ay sólo entonces!,
miré la trama lívida de la muerte y temblando
      rogué a solas por él.

Y el niño vio la cara tras la pared: sus manos
   se hundieron en las olas cerosas: la agonía
      hizo caer el sol entre sus sienes.
   Y desde su cabeza vi el canasto escarlata
de la serpiente negra, y entre el humo del rostro
      los anillos de fuego.

          Entonces,
   cuando a sus pies el rostro centelleaba,
          ¡ay sólo entonces!,

ELEGY FOR A DEAD BOY

And the child opened his eyes in the night, and the feathers
of death grazed his heart: the fever
sang over the threads of his veins
and I saw corrosive fingers on his mouth
and a slash that cut crooked across
the whole stem of his pulse.

Then
when down from the sky the wind came close,
oh, only then!
I prayed for him alone.

And the boy burned in the night, and the livid nails
sank into the tender flesh: over his eyes
the last stars glistened.
And I saw green teeth gnawing the virgin marrow
and in the center of his chest
all the leaves of his blood crumbled.

Then
when the thunderclap cut through the shadows,
oh, only then!
I looked on the purple deceit of death and trembling
I prayed for him alone.

And the child saw the face behind the wall: his hands
sank into the wax waves: the agony
pulled the sun down between his temples.
And from his head I saw the scarlet basket
of the black serpent, and in the smoke of his brow
circles of fire.

Then
when to his feet his face flashed,
oh, only then!

besé la tierna frente y el final de sus ojos,
          y solitariamente arrodillado
             rogué a solas por él.

Y las bocas solares del delirio soplaron
en la frente del niño, y el país de la muerte
          fue del tamaño de su corazón.
Y oí como en la noche respiraba y subía
desde el gélido rostro, toda la edad del viento,
             toda la eternidad.

                 Entonces,
cuando en la noche los barcos zarpaban,
             ¡ay sólo entonces!,
miré las velas rígidas en medio del espacio,
y rodeado de todas las lluvias siderales
             rogué a solas por él.

Y en el centro del mundo nos quedamos los últimos,
          y devastó su cuerpo el soplo que ascendía
             solitario, dejándome en lo oscuro.
Y me encontré en el nunca con el niño de entonces,
          y sobre las fronteras baldías de la noche
             rogué a solas por él.

                 Entonces,
          cuando el amanecer en mí soplaba,
             ¡ay sólo entonces!,
entre el viento del génesis y el trueno de la gloria,
          vi sus ojos fulgentes y su boca llameante,
          y en la mitad del ciclo terrible del silencio
             rogó él solo por mí.

I kissed his soft forehead and last his eyes,
and turning to myself I kneeled
and prayed for him alone.

And the sun's mouth blazing delirium blew
upon the face of the child. The country of death
had the shape of his heart
and I heard how in the night all the ages of the wind
all eternity sighed and slipped back
from his frigid brow.

Then
when in the night the boats put to sea,
oh, only then!
I saw the rigid sails slide into the void
and wholly encircled by the astral rain
I prayed for him alone.

And in the center of the world we were the last,
and the single breeze that blew laid waste his body
leaving me in the dark.
I found myself in never with the child of then
and over the untilled acres of the night
I prayed for him alone.

Then
when the dawn blew upon me,
oh, only then!
Between the winds of genesis and the thunder of revelation
I saw his brilliant eyes and his mouth calling
and in the middle of the terrible circle of silence
he prayed alone for me.

EL NINO IDIOTA

El niño idiota va en el bus repleto.
  Su madre no lo mira.
Ya no ve la saliva que le llaga
  y le cuelga perdida.
Pero el niño pregunta: "¿Qué me pasa?"
  "¡Cállate, niño!"

Al niño idiota lo han dejado solo
  con un ratón por compañía.
Y el ratón se ha subido por el puente
  de la saliva,
y poco a poco, tan poquito a poco,
  la mano le roía.
Pero el niño pregunta: "¿Qué me pasa?"
  "Déjame comer, niño."

El niño idiota ha visto que del cielo
  desciende el cáncer de las cenizas.
  Y salta de la órbita su ojo,
  y el niño idiota mira
ese ciego planeta que en su mano
    gira y gira.
Y no hay nadie que pueda responderle,
  no hay nadie que le diga
por qué su ojo ha estallado de repente
y por qué esta cubierto de saliva.

¿Quién le responde? ¡A ver!: ¿Quién le responde
  al niño idiota,
  al niño?

THE IDIOT CHILD

The idiot child rides on the crowded bus.
    His mother doesn't look at him
Doesn't see the saliva that runs
    and hangs lost.
But the child asks: "What's wrong with me?"
    "Shut up, kid!"

They have left the idiot child alone
    with a mouse for company
And the mouse has climbed up by the bridge
    built of saliva
Little by little, inch by inch
    gnaws at his hand.
But the child asks: "What's wrong with me?"
    "Let me eat, boy!"

The idiot child has seen how from the heavens
    falls the cancer of ashes
and his eye leaps out of its orbit
    and the idiot child looks
at that blind planet spinning in his hand.
And there is no one who can answer him,
    no one to tell him
    why his eye has suddenly burst
    why it's covered with spit.

Who answers him? Let's see: Who answers
    the idiot child,
        the child?

EFRAÍN BARQUERO

Translated by
MILLER WILLIAMS

Efraín Barquero, born in 1931, has recently returned from reading his poetry in China and
Russia. He is the author of several books from
which a large number of poems have appeared
in anthologies throughout Latin America and
which have been translated into both Russian
and English. He writes with a strong lyrical
line that moves forward with the insistence of
the best conversational prose. His poems carry
the reader through a private but perfectly com-
municated logic to that insight which is the
end of all poems.

MI AMADA ESTÁ TEJIENDO

Mi amada está tejiendo en la ventana.
Está tejiendo una inmensa mariposa.
Me mira en silencio, y yo la miro,
pensando en el hijo que volará sobre ella,
sintiendo lo bello que es haber luchado juntos,
tejiendo con nuestras manos una enredadera,
para que suba aquél más alto que nosotros.

Mi amada está tejiendo en la ventana.
Toda la tierra está tejiendo con ella,
la mariposa verde de la primavera.
Todo el mar está tejiendo con ella,
la ola blanca que limpiará los cielos.
Todos los hombres están tejiendo con ella,
la palabra que aromará la vida.

Mi amada está tejiendo en la ventana.
Me mira en silencio, y yo la miro;
contemplándonos los rostros tan queridos,
examinándonos las manos laboriosas;
pansando en las hojas que tiene en su regazo
para abrigar ese fruto milagroso;
pensando en las alas que tiene a medio hacer,
para que vuele el hijo como un pájaro,
hacia donde nosotros no alcancemos!

MY BELOVED IS KNITTING

My beloved is knitting at the window.
She is knitting an immense butterfly.
She looks at me in silence, and I look at her,
thinking of the son that will fly above her,
feeling the beauty in our fighting together,
knitting with our hands a climbing plant
until it goes up higher than we are.

My beloved is knitting at the window.
The whole earth is knitting with her
the green butterfly of the spring.
All the sea is knitting with her
white waves to wash down the sky.
All women are knitting with her
the word that gives life its smell.

My beloved is knitting at the window.
She looks at me in silence, and I look at her;
full of love our faces study us
and busy our hands examine us;
thinking of the leaves she has in her lap
to shelter that miraculous fruit;
thinking of the wings she has half-done
for our son to fly like a bird
where we cannot catch him.

LA MIEL HEREDADA

Mi abuelo era el río que fecundaba esas tierras.
Lleno de innumerables manos y ojos y oídos.
Y, al mismo tiempo, ciego y taciturno como un árbol.
Era la barba antigua y la voz profunda de la casa.
Era el sembrador y el fruto. La cepa rugosa.
El índice del tiempo y la sangre propicia.
Mi abuelo era el invierno con las manos floridas.
Era el propio río que poblaba las tierras.
Era la propia tierra que moría y renacía.

Mi abuela era la rama curvada por los nacimientos.
Era el rostro de la casa sentado en la cocina.
Era el olor del pan y la manzana guardada.
Era la mano del romero y la voz del conjuro.
Era la pobreza de los largos inviernos
envuelta en azúcar como humilde golosina.
Quince hijos comían de sus manos milagrosas.
Quince hijos dormían con su sueño de águila.
Muchos nietos y biznietos hemos seguido pasando
por sus brazos enjutos.
Pero ella es siempre la mano que mezcla agua y harina.
Es el silencio de la noche de pájaros dormidos.
Es el brasero de la infancia con la tortilla corredora.

Mi padre era el que más se parecía a la tierra.
Debe haber nacido junto con el maíz y el trigo.
Mi padre era moreno, y dormía en su caballo.
Era como el jinete lento de la primavera.

Mis otros tíos todos se parecían a las aves del lugar.
Todos tenían algo de los árboles y las serranías.
Algunos eran poderosos como los caballos percherones.
Otros tenían rostro de piedra o de trigo tostado.

THE INHERITANCE

My grandfather was the river that brought life to this land.
Full of unnumbered hands and eyes and ears,
still blind and silent as a tree.
He was the old beard, the deep voice of the house.
He was the sower, the seed, the great hungry root,
he was the index of time and the proper blood.
My grandfather was the winter with green hands.
He was the river that peopled the land,
he was the land that died and was born again.

My grandmother was a branch curved by children.
In the kitchen she was the face of the house.
She was the smell of bread and the saved apples,
the hand of the magic root and the conjuror's voice.
The poverty of those long winters
wrapped in sugar like the humble sweets.
Fed fifteen children from her miraculous hands.
Slept fifteen children with her sleep of owls.
Great grandsons have passed through her withered arms
but she is still the hand mixing water and flour,
she is the silence of the night with sleeping birds,
the oven of childhood with the vanishing bread.

My father was the one most like the earth.
He had to be born and raised with wheat and corn.
My father was dark, and he slept on his horse
like the slow rider of the spring.

My uncles were like the birds around the place.
They belonged to the trees and the unplowed fields.
Some were as powerful as draft horses.
Others had faces of stone or roasted wheat.

Pero todos recordaban las cosas más cercanas a la tierra.
Era un enjambre turbulent que llenaba la casa.
Era una bandada de queltehues que anunciaba la lluvia.
Eran los zorzales que se robaban las cerezas.

Yo nací cuando eran viejos ya; cuando mi abuelo
tenía el pelo blanco, y la barba lo alejaba como niebla.
Yo nací cuando ardían las fogatas de mayo.
Y lo primero que recuerdo es la voz del río y de la tierra.

TE ANDAN SUENOS EN LOS OJOS

Te andan sueños en los ojos y cachorros en las piernas,
y no puedes descansar: te llama el agua,
te llamo yo para contarte tantas cosas,
te llama llorando el desgarrón de mi camisa,
te llama mi corazón aumentando el griterío,
pero no se te cae tu sonrisa de loza.

Para todo tienes tiempo, y para mí toda tu vida.
Para las aves tienes grano, y para mí todo tu cuerpo.
Para la casa tienes flores, y para mí todo tu encanto.
Para los sueños tienes hilo, y para mí todos tus hijos.

Nadie se queda con hambre: ni los animales:
ni mi corazón: ni mis invitados.
Todos se llevan una hora tuya
y yo me llevo cada vez tu vida.

Me pregunto: ¿qué se llevaría la muerte,
si viniera ahora a buscarte?
Algo, tal vez, pero no todo.

But they all suggested something close to the earth.
It was a turbulent swarming that filled the house.
It was a flock of birds announcing rain.
A flurry of thrushes robbing the cherry trees.

They were already old when I was born.
My grandfather's hair was white
And the beard made him distant like the fog.
The fires of May were burning when I was born
and the first thing I can remember
is the voice of the river and the land.

DREAMS RUN IN YOUR EYES

Dreams run in your eyes and small dogs in your legs
and you can't rest: water calls you,
I call you to tell you things,
the rip in my shirt calls you crying,
my heart calls you adding to the uproar
but your china smile never falls.

You have time for everything, and for me your life.
You have grain for the birds, and for me your body.
You have flowers for the house, and for me your magic.
You have thread for dreams, and for me your sons.

No one is left hungry: not the animals
nor my heart nor my guests.
Each one takes away an hour
and I take every time your life.

I ask myself: what could death take
if he came now to get you?
Something, maybe, but not everything.

ROLANDO CÁRDENAS

Translated by
MILLER WILLIAMS

Rolando Cárdenas was born in Punta Arenas, near the southern tip of Chile, in 1933. He was educated at the State Technical University in Santiago as a Civil Engineer. His books have received two national awards for the quiet poems always about the people and the hard, white land of the far South.

TIERRA DEL FUEGO

La he mirado desde los caprichosos montes
de la península de Brunswick,
y se parece a una larga mancha azul
como si atardeciera el horizonte.
Si los antiguos navegantes de hace cuatro siglos
volvieran a atravesar su Estrecho,
aún verían parpadear fogatas en la noche
cuando los indios se ocupaban en quemar las matas
para fecundar la tierra de nuevo
o anduvieran de caza en sus canoas de troncos labrados a machete.

Muchas veces se han enrojecido las hojas del roble
y la luna ha cambiado de forma
mientras se endurecía el agua y el aire
desde que despertó el hondo sueño de sus raíces.
El viento del oeste la recorría entera
modelando la meridional estatura del Darwin,
sus riscos más pequeños y sus costas,
con un dolor obscuro.
De su corteza se desprendía una niebla blanca
como una barba o un perfume espeso
de tierra recién abierta a una lluvia sin tardanza.

El mar es la gran muralla que la circunda,
y no hay otro rumor más poderoso,
otro estruendo desenfrenada y único
como cuando se rompe en los acantilados.
Tiembla el mar abajo, majestuosamente,
y a las estrellas les palpita su agua.

El día se precipita con sus cuatro estaciones
y despierta con chillidos de pájaros marinos.
Rostro de piedra tiene
o simplemente blanco,

TIERRA DEL FUEGO

I have looked at it from the tricky mountains
of Brunswick Peninsula
and it seemed a great blue haze
as if evening were forming on the horizon.
If the old sailors of four centuries ago
were to return and sail this strait
they would still see blinking fires in the night
where the Indians busied themselves burning shrubs
to make the land fruitful again
or went hunting in their canoes
chopped out of trees.

Many times, since the roots have wakened from their dream,
the leaves of the oak have turned red
and the moon has changed its shape
while water and air grew hard.

The wind from the west would pass over
telling the lay of the land and the longitude of the Darwin,
of its smallest cliffs and coasts,
with an obscure pain.
Out of the bark came a white fog
like a beard or a heavy perfume
of recently opened earth in a punctual rain.

The sea is the grand encircling rampart
and there is no other sound more powerful —
no other wanton, no other single clamor
as when it shatters on the sheer rocks.
Underneath, the sea trembles majestically,
and the stars shimmer on the water.

The day pushes its four seasons forward,
wakes to seabirds screaming.
It has a face of stone,
or only white,

antiquísimo rostro de tierra roja,
anterior al sol y a la luna,
cuando sus montañas aún eran famosos cazadores.
La soledad le sopla sin descanso,
el cielo crece y no le arranca su misterio,
tal como la vieron los navegantes hace cuatro siglos.

Hacia el sur se acercan sus fogatas,
hacia donde la noche o el día permanecen por largos meses.

MUELLES

Reaparecen las despedidas.
Alguien dejó olvidadas las palabras de siempre
junto a la madera y los fierros.
Los muelles también quieren marchar
con sus gaviotas y sus grúas enormes.

Un homo negro hace más obscura el agua.

Cae un verano tibio sobre el último puerto.
Lejos, junto a los muelles rotos,
yacen oxidados esqueletos de barcos
sacudidos por un mar espeso.
El tiempo echa raíces en sus costados.
Las leyendas isleñas se repiten por las noches.
Resucitan iluminados bajo la tormenta
y como extraños espectros deformes
navegan de nuevo los canales.

Un pitazo hace volar más alto las gaviotas.
Esta mañana apenas existe.
Se aleja igual que palabras confusas.

Cuando atrás ya no queden contornos
y sólo podamos ver con el pensamiento,
la Cruz del Sur
señalará el camino del Estrecho.

an ancient face rising from the red earth
before the sun and the moon
when its mountains were still great hunters.

The solitude never resting, blows upon it.
The sky grows, and never uncovers the mystery:
so the navigators saw four centuries ago.

The fires draw together toward the south,
toward where the night, or the day, endures
through the long months.

WHARVES

Again the goodbyes.
Someone has left the customary words
forgotten on the wood and the iron.
The wharves, with their gulls and the great derricks,
might also leave.

A black smoke rises and the water turns dark.

A tepid summer falls on the last port.
Near the distant, battered wharves
rusty skeletons are shaken by the sea.
Time sticks roots in their sides.
By night the island legends are told again.
They come back, illuminated by the storm,
and like misshapen specters
sail the channels again.

A whistle and the gulls fly higher.
The morning, barely existing,
falls away like confused words.
When there are no contours left
and we can only see with our thoughts,
the Southern Cross
will light us through the strait.

LUISA JOHNSON

Translated by
MILLER WILLIAMS

Luisa Johnson, a native of Santiago, is in the
process of editing an Anthology of Brazilian
Romantic Poetry. The first collection of her
own work, *Horario de un Caracol*, was published in 1963. Miss Johnson's work is clearly
a woman's poetry, and at the same time bold,
often reckless, in the chances it takes.

NOTICIA

Las campanas de una iglesia
baten a viento y a sol,
golpean los badajos
en la humedad de la mañana,
porque con seguridad
alguien ha muerto, olvidando
su reloj sobre la mesa,
abandonando a su mujer
en cuarto oscuro,
dejando a sus niños
en desorden tan extraño.
Con seguridad alguien ha muerto,
lo dice el aire frío
que entorna largamente mi rostro,
haciéndome pensativa.

Ya tiene una palada negra sobre los ojos,
una palada, no de tierra sino de párpados.
Sí, creo que alguien murió.
Nada me dice que esto acontece:
el cielo se curva azul como en cada día,
la panadería calienta sus dedos fragantes.
Todo se allana al despertar.

Yo me visto en mi cuarto.
El viento penetra puro de olores.
Me siento ante el espejo,
me abulto en el espejo,
y sin embargo muy lejos en mi yo sé
que, mientras regresa la mañana,
alguien ha muerto;
con seguridad alguien ha muerto,
olvidándose de todo.

NOTICE

The bells of a church
batter the wind and the sun
the clappers hammer
in the moist air of the morning
because someone has died
forgetting his watch on the table
deserting his wife in a dark room
leaving his children
in that strange disorder.
Someone has died.
The cold air tells it
wrapping around my face
with these cold thoughts.

A shovelful is already on his eyes
not of earth but of eyelids.
Someone has died,
but nothing tells me so:
the sky moves in a blue arc
as it does every day
the bakery warms its fragrant fingers
everything moves together toward waking up.

Here in my apartment I'm getting dressed.
The wind comes in, pure and smelling of nothing.
I sit at the mirror,
grow large in the mirror,
and still I know
that while the morning returns
someone has died:
that someone has put it all
out of his mind.

HORAS

Quizá ya sea tiempo
de acordarse de la tarde.

Ya debe ser hora
de cerrar postigos
y encender una luz
disimulada en la casa,
y achicar el juego de los niños
bajo algún alero.

Es hora de enternecerse
sobre la última cebolla del dia
teñida de arreboles
y repartir fragancias en la casa
dando a la sopa ese olor atardecido.

Cuando callan los pájaros
bueno sería detener
el tumulto interminable de nuestro corazón
estar alertas
al juego del viento en las cortinas
transformándolas en compañeras.

Porque ante tanta distracción
¿qué ojos guardamos para palpar
el momento en que se va el sol?

DEVOTIONAL

Maybe the time has come
to be reconciled to the evening

It must be about the hour
for closing shutters
turning on a surreptitious light
and quieting the children
at play

It's the hour to be moved to pity
by the last onion of the day
stained by the red clouds
time to spread fragrances in the house
giving to the soup that odor of evening
When the birds quiet down
it would be good
to hold back the interminable tumult of our hearts
to be alert
to the play of wind in the curtains
transforming them into companions

because before such distraction
what eyes do we keep for groping
the moment when the sun goes?

ENRIQUE LIHN

Translated by
MILLER WILLIAMS

Enrique Lihn was born in Santiago in 1929
and studied at the University of Chile. He has
published several books of poems and short
stories. He received the Primer Premio de los
Juegos de Poesia in 1954, and *La Pieza Oscura,*
a book of poems published in 1963, won every
important prize around for that year. Lihn's
poetry is provincial in the best sense of the
word: he writes, to a greater extent perhaps
than do any of his contemporaries, in the
Chilean idiom. But if his poetry knows where
its home is, there is nothing provincial about
its audience. No young writer anywhere in
Spanish America is more read today or more
highly respected.

MONOLOGO DEL VIEJO CON LA MUERTE

Y bien, eso era todo.
Aquí tiene la vida, mírese en ella como en un espejo,
empáñela con su último suspiro.
Este es Ud. de niño, entre otros niños de su edad;
¿se reconocería a simple vista?
Le han pegado en la cara, llora a lágrima viva,
le han pegado en la cara.

Allí está varios años después, con su abuelo
frente al primer cadáver de su vida.
Llora al viejo, parece que llora
pero es más bien el miedo a lo desconocido.
El vuelo de una mosca lo distrae.

Y aquí vienen sus vicios, las pequeñas alegrías de un
            cuerpo reducido a su mínima expresión,
quince años de carne miserable;
y las virtudes, ciertamente, que luchan
con gestos más vacíos que ellas mismas.
Un gran amor, la perla de su barrio
le roba el corazón alegremente
para jugar con él a la pelota.
El seminario, entonces,
le han pegado en la cara. Ud. pone la otra;
pero Dios dura poco, los tiempos han cambiado
y helo aquí cometiendo una herejía.
Véase en ese trance, eso era todo:
asesinar a un muerto que le grita: no existo.
Existen a Marx y el diablo.

Recuerde, ese es Ud. a los treinta años;
no ha podido casarse
con su mujer, con la mujer de otro.

MONOLOGUE
OF THE OLD MAN WITH DEATH

And so that was all
Here is your life, look at yourself as you would look in a mirror.
Cloud it with your last breath.
Here you are as a child with other children your age;
Would you know yourself on sight?
They've hit him in the face, cries pitifully,
They've hit him in the face. He cries.

There, with his grandfather, years later,
Before the first corpse of his life
He mourns the old man, seems to mourn him,
More likely the fear of the unknown.
A fly distracts him.

And here come his vices, the poor joys of a body
Reduced to its minimum expression,
Fifteen years of miserable flesh;
And the virtues, naturally, which fight
With gestures emptier than they are.

A great love, the pearl of her neighborhood
Brightly steals his heart for a plaything.
The seminary then.
They hit him in the face. You give them the other;
But God doesn't last long, times have changed
And here we have him committing a heresey.
See yourself in that trance, nothing more:
Murder a corpse that screams: I don't exist.
Marx and the devil exist.

Remember, there you are at thirty;
You have not been able to marry
Your woman, the wife of another.

Vive en un subterráneo, en una cripta
de lo que se lo ofrece, sin oficio,
esqueléticamente, como un santo.
Del otro mundo viene ciertas noches
a visitarlo el padre de su padre:
—Vuelve sobre tus pasos, hijo mio, renuncia
al paraíso rojo que te chupa la sangre.
Total, si el mundo cambia a cañonazos,
antes que nada morirán los muertos.
Piensa en ti mismo, instala tu pequeño negocio.
Todo empieza por casa.

Mírese bien, es Ud. ese hombre
que remienda su única camisa
llorando secamente en la penumbra.
Viene de la estación, se ha ido alguien,
pero no era el amor, sólo una enferma
de cierta edad, sin hijos, decidida a olvidarlo
en el momento mismo de ponerse en marcha.
Ud. se pone en su lugar. No sufre.
¿Eso era el amor? Y bien, sí, era eso.
Tranquilo. Una mujer de cierta edad. Tranquilo.
Mírela bien, ¿quién era? Ya no la reconoce,
es ella, la que odia sus calcetines rotos,
la que le exige y le rechaza un hijo,
la que finge dormir cuando Ud. llega a casa,
la que le espanta el sueño para pedirle cuentas,
la que se ríe de sus libros viejos,
la que le sirve un plato vacío, con sarcasmo,
la que amenaza con entrar de monja,
la que se eclipsa al fin entre la muchedumbre.

Y bien, eso era todo. Véase Ud. de viejo
entre otros viejos de su edad, sentando
profundamente en una plaza pública.
Agita Ud. los pies, le tiembla un ojo,

You live in a cellar, a crypt
On what is offered, having no position,
Like a skeleton, a saint.
On certain nights from the other world
His father's father comes to visit him:
—Turn back, my son, renounce
The red paradise that sucks your blood.
Anyway, if the world is changed by cannon
Before all else the dead will die.
Think of yourself, open your little shop.
Everything starts at home.

Observe well, you are that man
Who mends his only shirt
Crying dryly in the half-light.
You come from the station, someone has left.
But it was not love, only a sick woman
Of some years, without children, set on forgetting you
At the very moment of her departure.
You put yourself in her place. She does not suffer.
That was love? So all right, it was.
Be still. A woman of some years. Be still.
Study her well. Who was she? Still you fail to recognize her,
It is she, who hates the holes in your socks.
Who demands and refuses a child,
Pretending to be asleep when you come home,
Who startles you awake to ask for explanations,
Who laughs at your old books,
Who serves you an empty plate, with sarcasm,
Who threatens to become a nun,
Who disappears at last into the multitude.

And so, that was all. See yourself an old man
With other old men your age, sitting
Profoundly in the public square,
You shake your feet, your eye twitches,

lo evitan las palomas que comen a sus pies
el pan que Ud. les da para atraérselas.
Nadie lo reconoce, ni Ud. mismo
se reconoce cuando ve su sombra.
Lo hace llorar la música que nada le recuerda.
Vive de sus olvidos
en el abismo de una vieja casa.
¿Por qué pues no morir tranquilamente?
¿A qué viene todo esto?
Basta, cierre los ojos;
No se agite, tranquilo, basta, basta.
Basta, basta, tranquilo, aquí tiene la muerte.

GALLO

Este gallo que viene de tan lejos en su canto,
iluminado por el primero de los rayos del sol;
este rey se plasma en mi ventana con su corona viva, odiosamente,
no pregunta ni responde, grita en la Sala del Banquete
como si no existieran sus invitados, las gargolas
y estuviera más solo que su grito.

Grita de piedra, de antigüedad, de nada,
lucha contra mi sueno pero ignora que lucha;
sus esposas no cuentan para él ni el maíz que en la tarde lo hará
   besar el polvo.
Se limita a aullar como un hereje en la hoguera de sus plumas.
Y es el cuerno gigante
que sopla la negrura al caer al infierno.

The pigeons at your feet avoid you
Pecking at the crumbs you entice them with.
Nobody knows you, not even you
Looking at your shadow.
You cry at music that has no memories
You live on your oblivions
In the abyss of an old house.
Then why not die in peace?
What does all this come to?
Enough, close your eyes;
Don't fret, be quiet, enough, enough.
Enough, enough, be still, here is your death.

ROOSTER

This rooster, come from some far place singing,
brightened by the first rays of the sun,
this king that molds himself at my window
with a living crown
hatefully
neither asks nor answers
screams in the Banquet Room
as if his guests the gargoyles did not exist
and he were more alone than his cry is.

He cries of stone, of antiquity, of nothing,
fights my sleep, ignoring what he fights.
His wives count for nothing, nor the corn
that in the evening he will kiss the dust for.
He howls like a heretic in the bonfire of his feathers.
He is a gigantic horn blowing the darkness to hell.

CEMENTERIO DE PUNTA ARENAS

Ni aun la muerte pudo igualar a estos hombres
que dan su nombre en lápidas distintas
o lo gritan al viento del sol que se los borra:
otro poco de polvo para una nueva ráfaga.
Reina aquí, junto al mar que iguala al mármol,
entre esta doble fila de obsequiosos cipreses
la paz, pero una paz que lucha por trizarse,
romper en mil pedazos los pergaminos fúnebres
para asomar la cara de una antigua soberbia
y reírse del polvo.

Por construirse estaba esta ciudad cuando alzaron
sus hijos primogénitos otra ciudad desierta
y uno a uno ocuparon, a fondo, su lugar
como si aún pudieran disputárselo.
Cada uno en lo suyo para siempre, esperando,
tendidos los manteles, a sus hijos y nietos.

GRAVEYARD AT PUNTA ARENAS

Not even death could turn these men to equals
who give their names on separate tablets of stone
or scream them into the wind that erases them:
a little more dust for a new gust of air.
Here rules, together with the sea that levels the marble
between this double row of obsequious cypresses
peace, but a peace that strains to shatter itself,
to break into a thousand pieces the dark diploma
to show the face of an old arrogance
and laugh at the dust.

This city was being built
when its first-born sons built another deserted city
and one by one, they took their places deeply
as if there were those who might not let them stay.
Each one within his own forever, waiting,
the table spread, for his sons and grandsons.

PABLO NERUDA

Translated by
CINNA LOMNITZ

Pablo Neruda, born in 1904, has been at various times a senator, a Chilean consul in Ceylon, Java, Spain, and Mexico. The best-known living writer in his language, he is often mentioned for the Nobel Prize. His books include *Veinte Poemas de Amor, Residencia en la Tierra, Estravagaria*, and many others.

AL PIE DESDE SU NINO

El pie del niño aún no sabe que es pie,
y quiere ser mariposa o manzana.

Pero luego los vidrios y las piedras,
las calles, las escaleras,
y los caminos de la tierra dura
van enseñando al pie que no puede volar,
que no puede ser fruto redondo en una rama.
El pie del niño entonces
fué derrotado, cayó
en la batalla,
fué prisionero,
condenado a vivir en un zapato.

Poco a poco sin luz
fué conociendo el mundo a su manera,
sin conocer el otro pie, encerrado
explorando la vida como un ciego.

Aquellas suaves uñas
de cuarzo, de racimo,
se endurecieron, se mudaron
en opaca substancia, en cuerno duro,
y los pequeños pétalos del niño
se aplastaron, se desequilibraron,
tomaron formas de reptil sin ojos,
cabezas triangulares de gusano.
Y luego encallecieron,
se cubrieron
con mínimos volcanes de la muerte,
inaceptables endurecimientos.

TO THE FOOT FROM HIS CHILD

The child's foot doesn't know he's a foot,
he wants to be a butterfly or an apple.

But broken glass and stones,
streets, flights of stairs,
and roads of the hard earth
go to teach a foot he can't fly,
can't be a round fruit on a branch.
So the child's foot
was defeated and fell
in battle,
was made prisoner,
sentenced to live in a shoe.

Little by little without light
he came to know the world in his own fashion,
Not knowing the other foot, shut in,
tapping his way through life like a blind man.

Those soft and tender nails
of quartz, of grape,
toughened, were changed
into an opaque stuff, a hardened horn,
and the small petals of the child
were squashed, lost symmetry,
took on shapes of reptiles without eyes,
triangular worms' heads.
And then they calloused,
grew over
with small volcano-marks of death,
unacceptable hardenings.

Pero este ciego anduvo
sin tregua, sin parar
hora tras hora,
el pie y el otro pie,
ahora de hombre
o de mujer,
arriba,
abajo,
por los campos, las minas,
los almacenes y los ministerios,
atrás,
afuera, adentro,
adelante,
este pie trabajó con su zapato,
apenas tuvo tiempo
de estar desnudo en el amor o el sueño,
caminó, caminaron
hasta que el hombre entero se detuvo.

Y entonces a la tierra
bajó y no supo nada,
porque allí todo y todo estaba oscuro,
no supo que había dejado de ser pie,
si lo enterraban para que volara
o para que pudiera
ser manzana.

But this blind fellow walked
without rest, without stopping
hour after hour,
that foot and the other foot,
now a man's
or a woman's,
up,
down,
across fields and mines,
grocery stores and ministries,
back,
outside, inside,
forward,
this foot labored with his shoe,
he barely found the time
to be undressed again in love or sleep,
he walked, they walked,
until the whole man stopped.

Then down into the ground
he went and knew no more,
for everything was dark there,
he never knew he was a foot no longer,
whether they buried him so that he'd fly,
or that he might
be an apple.

DÓNDE ESTARÁ LA GUILLERMINA?

Dónde estará la Guillermina?

Cuando mi hermana la invitó
y yo salí a abrirle la puerta,
entró el sol, entraron estrellas,
entraron dos trenzas de trigo
y dos ojos interminables.

Yo tenía catorce años
y era orgullosamente oscuro,
delgado, ceñido y fruncido,
funeral y ceremonioso:
yo vivía con las arañas,
humedecido por el bosque,
me conocían los coleópteros
y las abejas tricolores,
yo dormía con las perdices
sumergido bajo la menta.

Entonces entró la Guillermina
con dos relámpagos azules
que me atravesaron el pelo
y me clavaron como espadas
contra los muros del invierno.

Esto sucedió en Temuco,
Allá en el Sur, en la frontera.

Han pasado lentos los años
pisando como paquidermos,
ladrando como zorros locos,
han pasado impuros los años
crecientes, raídos, mortuorios,
y yo anduve de nube en nube,

WHERE IS GUILLERMINA?

I wonder where is Guillermina?

When my sister asked her over
and I went to open the door,
in came the sun, in came stars,
in came two pigtails of wheat
and two eyes that would never end.

I was fourteen
and proudly dark,
thin, stiff and frowning,
funereal and ceremonious;
I shared my life with the spiders,
dampened by the forest,
I was well known by the beetles
and by the three-colored bees,
I shared my bed with the partridges
drowning in mint.

In came Guillermina then
with two blue lightnings
that went through my hair
and nailed me like swords
to the winter walls.
This happened in Temuco,
way down South, on the frontier.

The slow years have gone by
stepping like pachyderms,
yelping like crazy foxes,
the impure years have gone by
growing, frayed, deathly,
and I wandered from cloud to cloud,

de tierra en tierra, de ojo en ojo,
mientras la lluvia en la frontera
caía, con el mismo traje.

Mi corazón ha caminado
con intransferibles zapatos,
y he digerido las espinas:
no tuve tregua donde estuve:
donde yo pegué me pegaron,
donde me mataron caí
y resucité con frescura,
y luego y luego y luego y luego,
es tan largo contar las cosas.

No tengo nada que añadir.

Vine a vivir en este mundo.

Dónde estará la Guillermina?

BESTIARIO

Si yo pudiera hablar con pájaros,
con ostras y con lagartijas,
con los zorros de Selva Oscura,
con los ejemplares pingüinos,
si me intendieran las ovejas,
los lánguidos perros lanudos,
los caballos de carretela,
si discutiera con los gatos,
si me escuchan las gallinas!

from land to land, from eye to eye,
while back on the frontier the rain
kept falling, with its changeless gown.

My heart has walked a road
with non-transferable shoes,
and I swallowed my share of thorns;
no truce reigned where I stopped;
I received the same blows I dealt,
and where I was killed I fell
and got up again,
and then and then and then and then,
it is a long story to tell.

I came to live in this world.

I wonder where is Guillermina?

BESTIARY

I wish I could talk with birds,
with the oyster or the lizards,
with the foxes in Selva Oscura,
with the exemplary penguins,
I wish sheep could understand me,
or the languid woolly dogs,
draught horses that pull the carts,
I wish that I argued with cats,
that hens would listen to me!

Nunca se me ha ocurrido hablar
con animales elegantes:
no tengo curiosidad
por la opinión de las avispas,
ni de las yeguas de carrera:
que se las arreglen volando,
que ganen vestidos corriendo!
Yo quiero hablar con las moscas,
con la perra recién parida
y conversar con las serpientes.

Cuando tuve pies para andar
en noche triples, ya pasadas,
seguí a los perros nocturnos,
esos escuálidos viajeros
que trotan viajando en silencio
con gran prisa a ninguna parte
y los seguí por muchas horas,
ellos desconfiaban de mí,
ay, pobres perros insensatos,
perdieron la oportunidad
de narrar sus melancolías,
de correr con pena y con cola
por las calles de los fantasmas.

Siempre tuve curiosidad
por el erótico conejo:
quiénes lo incitan y susurran
en sus genitales orejas?
Él va sin cesar procreando
y no hace caso a San Francisco,
no oye ninguna tontería:
el conejo monta y remonta
con organismo inagotable.
Yo quiero hablar con el conejo,
amo sus costumbres traviesas.

I never thought of speaking
to elegant animals:
I feel no curiosity
for the opinions of the wasps,
or of the racing mares:
let them get along in flight,
let them race and win their dresses!
I want to talk to the flics,
to the bitch-pup newly born,
to converse with the snakes.

When I still had feet to walk,
in triple nights, in times gone by,
I followed the nocturnal dogs,
those squalid travelers
that trot and trail in silence
with great haste towards nowhere,
and I followed them for hours,
they didn't trust me,
poor foolish dogs,
they missed the chance
to narrate their melancholics,
to run with grief and tail
through the streets of the ghosts.

I have always felt intrigued
about the erotic rabbit:
who incites him, whispering
in his long genital ears?
Ceaselessly he procreates
and pays no attention to St. Francis,
he does not listen to nonsense:
the rabbit mounts and dismounts
with untiring constitution.
I want to talk to the rabbit,
I am fond of his naughty customs.

Las arañas están gastadas
por páginas bobaliconas
de simplistas exasperantes
que las ven con ojos de mosca,
que la describen devoradora,
carnal, infiel, sexual, lasciva.
Para mí esta reputación
retrata a los reputadores
la araña es una ingeniera,
una divina relojera,
por una mosca más o menos
que la detesten los idiotas,
yo quiero conversar con la araña:
quiero que me teja una estrella.

Me interesan tanto las pulgas
que me dejo picar por horas,
son perfectas, antiguas, sánscritas,
son máquinas inapelables.
No pican para comer,
sólo pican para saltar,
son las saltarinas del orbe,
las delicadas, las acróbatas
del circo más suave y profundo:
que galopen sobre mi piel,
que divulguen sus emociones,
que se entretengan con mi sangre,
pero que alguien me las presente,
quiero conocerlas de cerca,
quiero saber a qué atenerme.

Con las rumiantes no he podido
intimar en forma profunda:
sin embargo soy un rumiante,
no comprendo que no me entiendan.
Tengo que tratar este tema

The spiders are worn trite
from pages of silliness
by exasperating simplists
who look at them through a fly's eyes,
who brand her as a devourer
carnal, faithless, sexual, lascivious.
To my mind this reputation
portrays the reputers:
the spider is an engineer,
a divine watchmaker,
for one fly's sake more or less
let idiots detest her,
I want to talk to the spider:
I want her to loom me a star.

Fleas interest me so much
I let them bite for hours,
they are perfect, ancient, sanscrit,
unappealable machines.
They never bite to eat,
they only bite to jump,
they are the jumpers of the earth,
the delicate, the acrobats
of a most soft, most deep circus;
let them gallop over my skin,
let them divulge their emotions,
let them have fun with my blood,
but let someone introduce them,
I want to know them closely,
I want to know where I stand.

With ruminants I have never
been intimate in a deep way:
yet I am a ruminant,
this incomprehension puzzles me.
I'll have to take up this matter

pastando con vacas y bueyes,
planificando con los toros.
De alguna manera sabré
tantas cosas intestinales
que están escondidas adentro
como pasiones clandestinas.

Qué piensa el cerdo de la aurora?
No cantan pero la sostienen
con sus grandes cuerpos rosados,
con sus pequeñas patas duras.

Los cerdos sostienen la aurora.

Los pájaros se comen la noche.

Y en la mañana está desierto
el mundo: duermen las arañas,
los hombres, los perros, el viento,
los cerdos gruñen, y amanece.

Quiero conversar con los cerdos.

Dulces, sonoras, roncas ranas,
siempre quise ser rana un día,
siempre amé la charca, las hojas
delgadas como filamentos,
el mundo verde de los berros
con las ranas dueñas del cielo.

La serenata de la rana
sube en mi sueño y lo estimula,
sube como una enredadera
a los balcones de mi infancia,
a los pezones de mi prima,
a los jazmines astronómicos
de la negra noche del Sur,
y ahora que ha pasado el tiempo
no me pregunten por el cielo:

while pasturing with cows and oxen,
while talking of plans with the bulls.
Somehow I shall be apprised
of many intestinal affairs
concealed inside
like clandestine passions.

What does the hog think of dawn?
They don't sing but they support it
with their large pink bodies,
with their small hard hooves.

The hogs hold up the dawn.

The birds eat up the night.

And at daybreak the world
is empty: spiders sleep,
men, dogs, the wind,
the hogs grunt, and it dawns.

I want to talk to the hogs.

Sweet, sonorous, raucous frogs,
I always wanted to be a frog some day,
I always loved the pond, the leaves,
thin and fine like filaments,
the green world of watercress,
with the frogs owning the sky.

The serenade of the frog
rises and stimulates my dream,
it rises like a climbing vine
to my balconies of childhood,
to the nipples of my cousin,
to the astronomic jasmine
of the black night of the South,
and now that time has gone by,
don't ask me about the sky:

pienso que no he aprendido aún
el ronco idioma de las ranas.

Si es así, cómo soy poeta?
Qué sé yo de la geografía
multiplicado de la noche?

En este mundo que corre y calla
quiero más comunicaciones,
otros lenguajes, otros signos,
quiero conocer este mundo.

Todo se han quedado contentos
con presentaciones siniestras
de rápidos capitalistas
y sistemáticas mujeres.
Yo quiero hablar con muchas cosas
y no me iré de este planeta
sin saber qué vine a buscar,
sin averiguar este asunto,
y no me bastan las personas,
yo tengo que ir mucho más lejos
y tengo que ir mucho más cerca.

Por eso, señores, me voy
a conversar con un caballo,
que me excuse la poetisa
y que el profesor me perdone,
tengo la semana ocupada,
tengo que oír a borbotones.

Cómo se llamaba aquel gato?

I think I have yet to learn
the hoarse language of the frogs.

If so, how am I a poet?
What do I know about the
manifold geography of night?

In this world of run and shut up
I want more communications,
other languages, other signs,
I do want to know this world.

Everyone has settled down
to sinister introductions
of swift capitalists
and systematic women.
I want to talk to many things
and I refuse to leave this planet
until I find out what I came looking for.
until I clear up this matter,
and people are not enough,
I have to go much farther,
and I have to go much closer.

Therefore, gentlemen, I go
to have a talk with a horse,
may the poetess excuse me
and the professor grant me leave,
I am busy all this week,
I have gushing tales to hear.

What was the name of that cat?

CIERTO CANSANCIO

No quiero estar cansado solo,
quiero que te canses conmigo.

Cómo no sentirse cansado
de cierta ceniza que qae
en las ciudades en otoño,
algo que ya no quiere arder,
y que en los trajes se acumula
y poco a poco cayendo
destiñendo los corazones.

Estoy cansado del mar duro
y de la tierra misterioso.
Estoy cansado de las gallinas:
nunca supimos lo que piensan,
y nos miran con ojos secos
sin concedernos importancia.

Te invito a que de una vez
nos cansemos de tantas cosas,
de los malos aperitivos
y de la buena educación.

Cansémonos de no ir a Francia,
cansémonos de por lo menos
uno o dos días en la semana
que siempre se llaman lo mismo
como los platos en la mesa,
y que nos levantan, a qué?
y que nos acuestan sin gloria.

Digamos la verdad al fin,
que nunca estuvimos de acuerdo

A CERTAIN WEARINESS

I don't want to be weary by myself,
I want you to be weary with me.

How can one help feeling weary
of certain ashes that fall
on cities in the fall,
a stuff that refuses to burn,
that gathers on suits
and drifts down by and by
and ends up by discoloring hearts.

I am weary of the hard sea
and of the mysterious earth.
I am weary of chickens:
we never learned what they think,
and they look at us dry-eyed
without paying any attention to us.

I invite you once and for all
to join me in being tired of many things,
of bad cocktails
and good breeding.

Let us tire of not going to France,
let us tire of at least
one or two days in the week
that are always called the same
like the dishes on the table,
and that wake us, for what?
and that bed us without glory.

Let us be true at last,
we had never agreed

con estos días comparables
a las moscas y a los camellos.

He visto algunos monumentos
erigidos a los titanes,
a los burros de la energía.
Allí los tienen sin moverse
con sus espadas en la mano
sobre sus tristes caballos.
Estoy cansado de las estatuas.
No puedo más con tanta piedra.

Si seguimos así llenando
con los inmóviles el mundo,
cómo van a vivir los vivos?

Estoy cansado del recuerdo.

Quiero que el hombre cuando nazca
respire las flores desnudas,
le tierra fresca, el fuego puro,
no lo que todos respiraron.
Dejen tranquilos a los que nacen!

Dejen sitio para que vivan!
No les tengan todo pensado,
no les lean el mismo libro,
déjenlos descubrir la aurora
y ponerle nombre a sus besos.

Quiero que te canses conmigo
de todo lo que está bien hecho.
De todo lo que nos envejece.
De lo que tienen preparado
para fatigar a los otros.

Cansémonos de lo que mata
y de lo que no quiere morir.

with these days to be compared
to the flies and the camels.

I have seen some monuments
to the memory of the titans,
of the mules of energy.
There they are kept motionless
with their sabers in their hands
sitting on their sorry horses.
I am tired of monuments.
I am worn down by so much stone.

If we keep replenishing
all the world with immobiles,
how shall the living live?

I am tired of memories.

I want man when he is born
to breathe the naked flowers,
the fresh soil, the pure fire,
not what everyone has breathed before.
Let alone those being born!
Make room for them to live!
Don't think their thoughts for them,
don't read them the same book,
let them discover the dawn
and give names to their kisses.

I want you to be weary with me
of everything well done.
Of everything that ages us.
Of what some keep in readiness
to wear the others down.

Let us be weary of all that kills
and of all that refuses to die.

LARINGE

Ahora va de veras dijo
la Muerte y a mí me parece
que me miraba, me miraba.

Esto pasaba en hospitales,
en corredores agobiados
y el médico me averiguaba
con pupilas de periscopio.
Entró su cabeza en mi boca,
me rasguñaba la laringe:
allí tal vez había caído
una semilla de la muerte.

En un principio me hice humo
para que la cenicienta
pasara sin reconocerme.
Me hice el tonto, me hice el delgado,
me hice el sencillo, el transparente:
sólo quería ser ciclista
y correr donde no estuviera.

Luego la ira me invadió
y dije, Muerte, hija de puta,
hasta cuándo nos interrumpes?
No te basta con tantos huesos?
Voy a decirte lo que pienso:
no discriminas, eres sorda
e inaceptablemente estúpida.

Por qué pareces indagarme?
Qué te pasa con mi esqueleto?
Por qué no te llevas al triste,
al cataléptico, al astuto,
al amargo, al infiel, al duro,

LARYNX

This time it's for good said Death
and I believe
he looked at me, he looked at me.

This happened in hospitals,
in disconsolate corridors,
and the doctor searched me with
the pupils of his periscope.
He poked his head inside my mouth,
he scratched and clawed at my larynx:
who knows, maybe a seed of death
had fallen there.

At first I tried to disappear
in the hope that the ashen one
would walk by without recognizing me.
Now I played dumb, now I played lean,
now I played simple and transparent:
all I wanted was to ride a bike
and run someplace where he wouldn't go.

But then my blood began to boil
and I said, Death, you son of a whore,
will you stop interrupting us?
Aren't you content with all those bones?
I'm going to tell you what I think:
you don't discriminate, you are deaf
and unacceptably stupid.

Why do you seem to poke at me?
What's my skeleton to you?
Why don't you take the gloomy one,
the cataleptic one, the shrewd,
the embittered, the faithless, the hard,

al asesino, a los adúlteros,
al juez prevaricador,
al mentiroso periodista,
a los tiranos de las islas,
a los que incendian las montañas,
a los jefes de policía
con carceleros y ladrones?
Por qué vas a llevarme a mí?
Qué tengo que ver con el cielo?
El infierno no me conviene
y me siento bien en la tierra.

Con estas vociferaciones
mentales me sostenía
mientras el Doctor intranquilo
se paseaba por mis pulmones:
iba de bronquio en bronquio como
pajarillo de rama en rama:
yo no sentía mi garganta,
mi boca se abría como
el hocico de una armadura
y entraba y salía el Doctor
por mi laringe en bicicleta
hasta que adusto, incorregible,
me miró con su telescopio
y me separó de la muerte.

No era lo que se creía.
Esta vez sí no mi tocaba.

Si les digo que sufrí mucho,
que quería al fin el misterio,
que Nuestro Señor y Señora
me esperaban en su palmera,
si les digo mi desencanto,
y que la anguistia me devora

the murderer, the adulterers,
the prevaricating judge,
the lying journalist,
the tyrants of the islands,
the people who burn mountains down,
the chiefs of police
with cops and robbers?
Why is it me you want to take?
What do I have to do with Heaven?
Hell is no place for me, I know,
and I'm quite well on earth.

With these vociferations
I sustained myself mentally
while the restless doctor was
taking walks inside my lungs;
from bronchus to bronchus
he jumped like a bird from branch to branch:
I had stopped feeling my own throat,
my mouth was gaping like
the snout of an armored knight
and the doctor came and went
through my larynx on a bicycle
until, austere, incorrigible,
he peered at me with his telescope
and separated me from death.

It was not what one might have thought.
This time it was not my turn.

If I tell you how I pined
to know at last the mystery,
how Our Lord and Lady both
were waiting for me on their palm tree,
If I tell you my disappointment,
and how by anguish I am consumed

de no tener muerte cercana,
si digo como la gallina
que muero porque no muero
denme un puntapié en el culo
como castigo a un mentiroso.

FÁBULA DE LA SIRENA Y LOS BORRACHOS

Todos estos señores estaban dentro
cuando ella entró completamente desnuda
ellos habían bebido y comenzaron a escupirla
ella no entendía nada recién salía del río
era una sirena que se había extraviado
los insultos corrían sobre su carne lisa
la inmudicia cubrío sus pechos de oro
ella no sabía llorar por eso no lloraba
no sabía vestirse por eso no se vestía
la tatuaron con cigarrillos y con corchos quemados
y reían hasta caer al suelo de la taberna
ella no hablaba porque no sabía hablar
sus ojos eran color de amor distante
sus brazos construídos de topacios gemelos
sus labios se cortaron en la luz del coral
y de pronto salió por esa puerta
apenas entró al río quedó limpia
relució como una piedra blanca en la lluvia
y sin mirar atrás nadó de nuevo
nadó hacia nunca más hacia morir.

because my death is not at hand,
if I say as the little hen said
that I am dying to be dead
then let me have a kick in the ass
as punishment for being a liar.

FABLE OF THE SIREN
AND THE DRUNKARDS

All these gentlemen were inside
when she walked in completely naked
they had been drinking and they began spitting on her
she understood nothing she came fresh from the river
she was a siren who was lost
the insults ran down her smooth flesh
the filth covered her breasts of gold
she did not know how to cry therefore she was not crying
she did not know how to dress therefore she was not dressed
they tattooed her with cigarettes and burnt corks
and they laughed till they dropped to the tavern floor
she did not speak because she did not know how to speak
her eyes were the color of faraway love
her arms constructed of twin topazes
her lips had been cut out of coral light
and at once she went out by that door
as soon as she entered the river she was cleaned
she shone like a white stone in the rain
and without looking back she swam again
swam towards nevermore towards dying.

NICANOR PARRA

Translated by
MILLER WILLIAMS

Nicanor Parra is introduced in his interview with Mr. Williams.

A TALK WITH NICANOR PARRA

NICANOR PARRA is one of the best-known poets writing in Spanish today. Perhaps it would be better to say, the Spanish of today. Because no one has done more to give the language the freedom of the streets, to push the language to its limits, than Parra has. And not even Vicente Huidobro was so much a symbol of decadence to his enemies or a cause célèbre to his defenders as Parra was after the publication of *Poems and Antipoems* in 1954.

Born in 1914 in Chillán, in the south of Chile, Parra grew up there, playing with his brothers and sisters around the school where his father taught, or about the stones of the village cemetery. His studies at the University of Chile were concentrated in mathematics and physics, which he continued to pursue at Brown University in Rhode Island and at Oxford. He is presently Professor of Theoretical Physics at the Insituto Pedagogico of the University of Chile, a position which has not prevented him from reading his poems and giving talks during the past few years in Peking, Moscow, Mexico City, Havana, Paris, and San Francisco. During the past year he was Visiting Professor at Louisiana State University.

In addition to *Poemas y Antipoemas*, his books include *Cancionero sin Nombre*, his first book, published in 1937, *La Cueca Larga*, in 1958, and *Versos de Salon* in 1962. City Lights published a selection under the title *Antipoems* in English and Spanish in 1960. New Directions will publish a larger and more representative group of poems this year. There are also translations in a number of other languages, including Finnish, French, and Russian.

Parra is quick-witted and amiable, generous with his time and his stories, and — like his antipoems — seems to have been chiseled out of a stone that shifts when we are not looking. There is this solidity, firmness of intellect about him, and at the same time an incredible chameleon whimsicalness that leaves one, after an evening in his rough-stone house overlooking Santiago, feeling good and exhausted.

This was the house my friends took me to, shortly after Parra had returned from a tour of Russia. I was meeting him for the first time, but it might have been the thousandth. In a very few minutes we were munching hard bread, pouring down the famous Chilean wine, and talking.

WILLIAMS

You are called a member of the generation of 1938. This would have you writing at least twenty-six years ago, certainly before you became a mathematician. What led you into the fields of mathematics and physics?

PARRA

An honest desire to be everywhere at once. It wasn't intellectual pride. It was an instinct for integration. But the whim is expensive, of course. The writers consider me a man of science, and my university colleagues look on me as a writer. And then there are reasons of a practical nature. The full-time poet doesn't have any place in our society. To survive in a so-called underdeveloped country, there's no choice but to be a one-man band.

WILLIAMS

Has your scientific training influenced your poetry? Is it in any way responsible for your particular images, or the hard feeling of your poems, the terseness?

PARRA

For the imagery, yes. As a student of the fundamentals of classical mechanics, I've formed the habit of taking a step only when I can see the road clearly. The historical-critical method of math, carried over consciously or unconsciously into the area of poetic investigation, can't help but end up in a clear, neat, and transparent expression. But sometimes the mechanism also works in reverse. I mean that the tool of antipoetry makes a good battering ram for trephining the skull of Newton, to see what went on inside. As a result of that trephination we have antimechanics, which explains the mystery of the equation $F=ma$, starting with a principle of identity of gravitational mass in terms of inertia.

WILLIAMS

Fernando Alegría has said that you are the only writer of your generation to form a "school." Is there in fact a surrealist school of poetry in Chile?

PARRA

Well, I don't identify myself with either the Chilean or the French surrealists, however much respect I may have for the psychoanalytic principle. I like the superficial psychical processes as much as the Freudian depths. I work with the integral human being. And not only as a psychological entity but also, and very significantly, as an historical entity. To quote — nothing which is human is foreign to me. That's why I'm not to be confused with the poets of beauty, who don't count for much in my book. I prefer to be called an antipoet. Also at one time or another in their development, Enrique Lihn — a great new figure in Chilean poetry, Raul Rivera, Gabriel Carvajal, Mario Ferrero, Armando Uribe and quite a few others have been called antipoets. Even the very Neruda, for his *Estravagario*. A book called *Antipoems 1962* written by Simón Kargieman has come out of Argentina. Among other writers who understand the meaning of the antipoem are Mario Benedetti of Uruguay, Carlos Rebolledo of Venezuela, Aristides Martinez of Panama, and Oscar Ichaza of Bolivia. And some North American poets, such as Ginsberg and Ferlinghetti and Luis Garcia. When I was in Russia I became friends with Vosnesensky, who is an antipoet through and through. Juan-Agustín Palazuelos is working now in an antiprose. The outstanding exegetes of antipoetry are Jorge Elliott, Lihn, Sergio Hernandez, Frederico Shopf, and Pedro Lastra of Chile, Benedetti and Rodriguez Monegal of Uruguay, Arthur Lundquist of Sweden, and Vidas Silimas of Russia. Its more irreconcilable enemies are Pablo de Rokha and the naïve Father Salvatierra.

WILLIAMS

Would you use the word "beat" to describe the antipoem? Or the antipoets?

PARRA

Well, you know the San Francisco beatniks have edited a collection of my antipoems. They're naturally interested in my work, since there are certainly common elements in our writing. To begin with, we are all irreducibly non-conformists. Beatniks and antipoets have great faith in laughter as the liberating force. But I'm not opposed to a bath, and I don't favor using marijuana.

WILLIAMS

Your poems are generally called "surrealistic." Certainly such poems as the "Soliloquio del Individuo" and "La Montaña Rusa" tell us clearly something of what you believe about the world. They are to some degree didactic. But "Sueños" appears to be purely surrealist imagery. How does this relate to your work as a whole?

PARRA

In "Sueños" I don't pretend anything more than the production of the sensations of sleep in a wide-awake reader, for which I avail myself of a simple method of projection of elementary dream situations in the way of a magic lantern. Maybe this is where I find myself nearest to realism. But as a rule my poetry dives into the state of wakefulness as often as into the land of dreams. Antipoetry shoots in all directions with the same force.

WILLIAMS

You use the number forty frequently. Does this have some special significance for you?

PARRA

I hadn't realized it. Possibly I took it from Spanish *brisca*, a card game I played a lot when I was a boy in a tough neighborhood in

Chillán. In brisca, forty — the horse and the trump king — is the winning combination.

WILLIAMS

Your poetry seems a clear turn away from the lyricism of Neruda. Since he lives at least part of the time on the coast, and you live here in Santiago, I wonder if the poem "Viva la Cordillera de los Andes," which says something like "Hail to the Andes Mountains, down with the coastal range," is an expression of your feelings about the new poetry and the more conventional work.

PARRA

There's a tendency to think of my acts and thoughts in terms of Neruda. Which is no surprise, since he constitutes perhaps the most natural and legitimate frame of reference in matters of Latin American poetic expression, to the point that some call me anti-Neruda. Those who have read "Discursos" [by Neruda and Parra, Nascimento Press, Stgo., 1962] know that there aren't deep divisions between us. Our relationship is one of father to son, and not Kafir to Hottentot. In matters of intellect and in affection this relation holds true. My verses aim at the negation which is necessarily implied in every emotional, categorical affirmation. They amount to a joyous acceptance of life and a humorous condemnation of death. Remember that in Chile the sun rises on the Andes and sets on the sea.

WILLIAMS

Nicanor Parra broke the mold of Spanish poetry, as Whitman broke it in English, and Pound again. Is this what you set out to do?

PARRA

Yes. It was a job that had to be done. We had to open the doors and windows of the Atheneum to let some light and oxygen in. We had to focus again on the flesh-and-blood man in all his dimensions, positive as well as negative. But my intention is still more drastic than Pound's, because I work with a chameleon that moves itself through all the colors of the spectrum. He's at the same time lucid and tenebrous, proletarian and bourgeois, sick and healthy. The only constant in my creation is authenticity.

WILLIAMS

There is what might be called an antipoetry being written in the States now — the prose-poem of Karl Shapiro and others. Are you familiar with it?

PARRA

No, I don't know Shapiro, but I'm going to sit down and read him immediately.

WILLIAMS

Was your early poetry fashioned after the traditional work of the Spanish masters?

PARRA

I began as a Garcialorquian poet. My working plan at that time was to apply to Chile the method Lorca had made his in Spain. But after a while I grew disillusioned with my master and I had to think out my own doctrine. Then, as I began to think for myself, the first thing I became aware of was that my character doesn't derive from the renaissance but from a lot further back. From Aristophanes. From Chaucer. From Gesta Romanorum. From the Spanish picaresque novel. From Cervantes. From Quevedo. And then from Kafka, and Chaplin. But the most important influence on the creation of the antipoem was the Chilean popular characters. Especially the Christ of Elqui and *el roto choro*. [The "Christ" was a sidewalk sage who roamed the byways of Chile; *el roto choro* is a hard-nosed, wisecracking tramp.]

WILLIAMS

I'm told you lived for a time in the home of Neruda, and I

know that you've been friends for years. Has he had any direct influence on the development of your poetry?

PARRA

I've never lived in Neruda's house. We've been friends, of course, and we still are friends. And we've lived in the same neighborhood. Sometimes we've seen each other daily. Neruda taught me many things. The road of every Spanish-speaking poet necessarily passes through "Residencia en la Tierra." But he's a grand gentleman and I'm a coarse country boy.

WILLIAMS

Who, excluding Nicanor Parra, are the best poets writing now in Latin America?

PARRA

I don't know current Latin American poetry that well, to be able to evaluate it. The Chilean poet who interests me most is Enrique Lihn.

WILLIAMS

Why is it that Chile has produced so much more than its share of good poets?

PARRA

Chile is a unique country for countless and permanent reasons. The first reason is her geography. As social and economic conditions improve, she will also produce a great number of prose writers, scientists, sages, philosophers.

WILLIAMS

Of the languages you speak — Spanish, French, and English, at least — how do they compare as mediums for poetic expressions? Does a poet have any advantage or disadvantage working in one rather than another?

As antipoetry is not a linguistic discipline, but a method of approximating reality through the magic of words, it follows as a matter of course that there are no privileged languages where it's concerned. There's nothing more appropriate to the Alacalufe Indian, for example, than the Alacalufe language. Incursions into other languages, of course, can bring the antipoet to unexpected panoramas. Otherwise Picasso wouldn't have been so interested in the plastic languages of primitive peoples. And I agree that one language may be more complex or richer than another, but often what is gained in extension is lost in intensity. But their study is helpful. For me, English has been a general source of very interesting suggestions.

WILLIAMS

What are the common weaknesses of Spanish poetry? That is to say, what are the ills Spanish poets most often fall prey to?

PARRA

Formalism and rhetoric, grandiloquence, posturing, preciosity, limpness of character, softness.

WILLIAMS

Finally, an antiquestion: What's the answer you would have given to some important question I haven't asked?

PARRA

That there is no poetry without liberty. That poetry is the soul of freedom expressed.

EL PEQUENO BURGUÉS

El que quiera llegar al paraíso
Del pequeño burgués tiene que andar
El camino del arte por el arte
Y tragar cantidades de saliva:
El noviciado es casi interminable.

Lista de lo que tiene que saber.

Anudarse con arte la corbata
Deslizar la tarjeta de visita
Sacudirse por lujo los zapatos
Consultar el espejo veneciano
Estudiarse de frente y de perfil
Ingerir una dosis de cognac
Distinguir una viola de un violín
Recibir en pijama a las visitas
Impedir la caída del cabello
Y tragar cantidades de saliva.

Todo tiene que estar en sus archivos.
Si su mujer se entusiasma con otro
Le recomiendo los siguientes trucos:
Afeitarse con hojas de afeitar
Admirar las bellezas naturales
Hacer crujir un trozo de papel
Sostener una charla por teléfono
Disparar con un rifle de salón
Arreglarse las uñas con los dientes
Y tragar cantidades de saliva.

Si desea brillar en los salones
El pequeño burgués
Debe saber andar en cuatro pies
Estornudar y sonreír a un tiempo

THE LITTLE MAN

Whoever wants to go to the little man's heaven
has to go the way of art for art's sake
and swallow great quantities of saliva:
The apprenticeship is almost endless.

Here is a list of what he will have to know:

How to fashion his necktie with a flair
how to slip a man a calling card
how to pop a shine on a pair of shoes
how to consult a Venetian mirror
to study himself in profile and full-face
how to take a shot of cognac
how to distinguish viola and violin
how to receive visitors in pajamas
how to slow the falling of his hair
and how to swallow great quantities of saliva.

He will need to have everything in his files.
If his wife is excited for someone else
I recommend the following:
shave with a razor
admire the natural beauties
crumple up a piece of paper
talk on the phone
shoot a pop-gun
pare the nails with the teeth
and swallow great quantities of saliva.

If he wants to shine at social gatherings
The little man
has to know how to run on four feet
to sneeze and smile at the same time
to waltz on the edge of a cliff
to deify the instruments of sex

Bailar un vals al borde del abismo
Endiosar a los órganos sexuales
Desnudarse delante del espejo
Deshojar una rosa con un lápiz
Y tragar toneladas de saliva.

A todo esto cabe preguntarse
¿Fué Jesucristo un pequeño burgués?

Como se ve, para poder llegar
Al paraíso del pequeño burgués
Hay que ser un acróbata completo:
Para poder llegar al paraíso
Hay que ser un acróbata completo.
¡Con razón el artista verdadero
Se entretiene matando matapiojos!
Para salir del círculo vicioso
Recomiendan el acto gratuito:

Aparecer y desaparecer
Caminar en estado cataléptico
Bailar un vals en un montón de escombros
Acunar un anciano entre los brazos
Sin despegar la vista de su vista
Preguntarle la hora al moribundo
Escupir en el hueco de la mano
Presentarse de frac en los incendios
Arremeter con el sortejo fúnebre
Ir más allá del sexo femenino
Levantar esa losa funeraria
Ver si cultivan árboles adentro
Y atravesar de una vereda a otra
Sin referencias ni al porqué ni al cuándo
Por la sola virtud de la palabra
Con su bigote de galán de cine
A la velocidad del pensamiento.

undress in front of a mirror
defoliate a rose with a pencil
and swallow great buckets of saliva.

After this you can ask yourself
Was Jesus Christ a little man?

You can see
if you want to get to the paradise
of the little man you have to be
a perfect acrobat.
If you want to get to paradise
you have to be a perfect acrobat.

No wonder the true artist
passes the time killing dragon flies!
To break out of the vicious circle
the gratuitous act is recommended:

to appear and disappear
to move in a cataleptic state
to waltz on a pile of debris
to rock an old man in your arms
never taking your eyes from the old man's eyes
to ask a dying man what time it is
to spit in the hollow of your hand
to follow fire trucks in a dinner jacket
to cut through funeral processions
to go further than the female sex
to lift up that tombstone
to see if trees are growing underneath
and then to cross from one side to the other
with neither reason nor a time
for the sake of changing
with the moustache of a movie hero
and the speed of thought.

MOMIAS

Una momia camina por la nieve
Otra momia camina por el hielo
Otra momia camina por la arena.

Una momia camina por el prado
Una segunda momia la acompaña.

Una momia conversa por teléfono
Otra momia se mira en un espejo.

Una momia dispara su revólver.

Todas las momias cambian de lugar
Casi todas las momias se retiran.

Varias momias se sientan a la mesa
Unas momias ofrecen cigarillos
Una momia parece que bailara.

Una momia más vieja que las otras
Da de mamar a su niño de pecho.

PIDO QUE SE LEVANTE LA SESION

Señoras y señores:
Yo voy a hacer una sola pregunta:
¿Somos hijos del sol o de la tierra?
Porque si somos tierra solamenta
no veo para qué
continuamos filmando la película:
Pido que se levante la sesión.

ZOMBIES

A zombie walks in the snow
Another zombie walks on ice
Another zombie walks along the shore.

A zombie walks through the meadow
A second zombie goes with her.

A zombie talks on the phone
Another zombie looks in a mirror.

A zombie fires a revolver.

All the zombies change places
Almost all of the zombies go to bed.

Several zombies sit at a table
Some offer the others cigarettes
A zombie seems to be dancing.

A zombie older than the others
puts her baby to suck.

I MOVE THE MEETING BE ADJOURNED

Ladies and gentlemen:
I have only one question:
Are we children of the sun or of the earth?
Because if we are only earth
I don't see why
we continue to film the picture:
I move the meeting be adjourned.

EN EL CEMENTERIO

Un anciano de barbas respetables
Se desmaya delante de una tumba.
El la caída se rompe una ceja.
Observadores tratan de ayudarlo:
Uno le toma el pulso
Otro le echa viento con un diario.

Otro dato que puede interesar:
Una mujer lo besa en la mejilla.

EL GALAN IMPERFECTO

Una pareja de recién casados
Se detiene delante de una tumba.
Ella viste de blanco riguroso.

Para ver sin ser visto
Yo me escondo detrás de una columna.

Mientras la novia triste
Desmaleza la tumba de su padre
El galán imperfecto
Se dedica a leer una revista.

IN THE GRAVEYARD

An old man with a respectable beard
faints in front of a tomb
Breaks open an eyebrow
The people around him try to help:
One takes his pulse
One fans him with a paper.

Another fact that may be of some interest:
A woman kisses him on the cheek.

THE IMPERFECT LOVER

A couple just married
stops at a grave.
Her dress is rigorous white.

To see without being seen
I hide behind a column.

While the sad bride
weeds the grave of her father
the imperfect gentleman concentrates
on reading his paper.

ALBERTO RUBIO

Translated by
MILLER WILLIAMS

Alberto Rubio was born in Santiago in 1928
and has traveled in Spain, France, and Italy.
His first book, *La Greda Vasija*, was very well
received, and the standard *Antologia de Poesia
Chilena Nueva* includes his work. His lines are
both lyrical and hard, always human and knowing, full of pathos and that necessary and terrible distance.

LA ABUELA

Se puso tan mañosa al alba fría,
la cerrada de puertas, la absoluta de espaldas,
cosiéndose un pañuelo que nadie conocía.

Se bajó bien los párpados. Con infinita llave
los cerró para siempre. Unos negros marinos
vinieron a embarcarla en una negra nave.

Y la nave, de mástiles de espermas y de velas
de coronas moradas de flores, era el barco
que lleva a extraños puertos a las hondas abuelas.

No hizo caso a nadie: ni a la hija mayor,
ni a su eterno rosario: tan mañosa se puso,
tan abuela recóndita metióse en su labor.

Ni el oleaje de rostros, ni la lléntea resaca
pueden ahora atraer su nave hasta esta costa:
¡ni nadie de su extraño pañuelo ahora la saca!

THE GRANDMOTHER

When the cold dawn came she grew cranky,
banging doors, turning her back,
sewing a shawl nobody recognized.

Her eyelids fell completely. With some eternal key
she closed them forever. Black sailors
carried her onto a black ship.

And the ship, its mast a candle, its sail
a crown of purple flowers, was the boat
to carry deep grandmothers to strange ports.

She didn't listen to anyone. Not the older daughter
nor the everlasting rosary. That was how cranky she was,
how grandmotherly she went about her business.

Now neither the wave of faces
nor the weeping surge of water on the sand
can draw the ship to this coast.
And nobody takes from her now her dark shawl.

RETRATO DE UNA NINA

Mi corazón se siente oblicuo ante esta niña.
Oblicuos son sus ojos, oblicuos son sus cejas,
y su frente perqueña es un cuadrado oblicuo,
y aguda su barbilla, se ladea oblicuándose.

Y viste un cerde oblicuo, el cerde de los ojos,
en dos alas oblicuas de mariposa oblicua.
Cuando levanta el viento, su vestido se alza
oblicuando los aires cuadradamente cerdes.

Los pómulos dorados le agudizan la cara,
ladeándola en exágono de ladeada tristeza.
Mi corazón se siente oblicuo ante esta niña,
se ladea dorádose, y verde, siente alas.

PORTRAIT OF A GIRL

My heart turns oblique in front of this girl.
Oblique are her eyes, oblique her brows,
her small forehead is an oblique square
and acute the chin obliquing itself tilts.

And dressed an oblique green, the green of her eyes
in two oblique wings of butterfly oblique.
When the wind rises, up lifts her skirt
obliquing the squarely green air.

The golden cheek bones give an acuteness to the face
tilting in a hexagon of tilted sadness.
My heart feels oblique in front of this girl
tilts gilding itself, and green. Feels wings.

JORGE TEILLIER

Translated by
MILLER WILLIAMS

Jorge Teillier was born in Lautaro in 1935. He
has published a number of books, and was
awarded the Premio Gabriela Mistral and the
Premio Municipal in 1961. He is the most
romantic of Chile's new poets, and will speak
of himself as belonging, in fact, to another
century. He is much read, nevertheless, and
well praised, in the century he was born to.

FIN DEL MUNDO

El dia del fin del mundo
será limpeo y ordeando
como el cuaderno
del mejor alumno del curso.
El borracho del pueblo
dormirá en una zanja,
el tren expreso pasará
sin detenerse en la estación
y la banda del regimento
ensayará infinitamente
la marcha que toca hace viente años en la plaza.
Sólo que algunos niños
dejarán sus volantines enredados
en los alambres telefónicos
para vovler llorando a sus casas
sin saber qué decir a sus madres,
y yo grabaré mis iniciales
en la corteza de un tilo
sabiendo que eso no sirve para nada.

Los amigos jugarán fútbol
en el potrero de las afueras.
Los evangélicos saldrán a contar a las esquinas.
La anciano loca paseará con quitasol.
Y yo diré para mi mismo: "El mundo no puede terminar
porque las palomas y los gorriones
siguen peleando por la avena en el patio."

END OF THE WORLD

The day the world ends
will be clean and orderly
like the notebook
of the best student in the class.
The town drunk
will sleep in a ditch,
the express train will pass
without stopping at the station
and the regimental band
will endlessly practice
the march they have played in the square
                    for twenty years.
Only some children
will leave their kites tangled
in telephone lines
to run home crying
not knowing what to tell their mothers
and I will carve my initials
in the bark of a linden tree
knowing that it won't do any good.

The kids will play football
in the empty lot on the edge of town.
The holy sects will come out
            to sing on the street corners.
The crazy old woman will pass by with her parasol.
And I will say to myself: "The world cannot end,
because here on the patio the pigeons and the sparrows
are still squabbling over the grain."

A UN NIÑO EN UN ARBOL

Eres el único habitante
de una isla que sólo tú conoces,
redeado del oleaje del viento
y del silencio rozado apenas
por el vuelo de una lechuza.

Ves un arado roto
y una trilladora cuyo esqueleto
permite un último relumbre del sol.
Ves al verano convertido en espantapájaros
cuyas pesadillas angustian los sembrados.
Ves la acequia
en cuyo fondo un amigo desaparecido
tiene el primer barco de papel que tú
        echaste a navegar.
Ves el pueblo y los campos extendidos
como las páginas de un libro de lectura
donde un día sabrás que leiste la historia de la
        felicidad.

El almacenero sale a cerrar los postigos.
Las hijas del granjero encierran las gallinas.
Ojos de extraños peces
miran amenazantes desde el cielo.
Hay que volver a tierra.
Tu perro viene a saltos a encontrate.
Tu isla se hunde en el mar de la noche.

TO A BOY IN A TREE

You are the sole inhabitant
of an island known only to you,
surrounded by waves of the wind
and a silence the flight of an owl
can barely stir.

You see a broken plow
and a threshing machine whose skeleton
gives a final luster to the sun.
You see how the summer is changed in the scarecrows
who haunt the field-hands, moaning their bad dreams.

You see the swamp.
In those waters a vanished friend
holds the first paper boat you put to sea.
You find the village and the farms
like the pages of a picture book.
One day you will know
how you read here the history of gladness.

The storekeeper closes the shutters.
The farmer's daughters put the chickens to roost.
Eyes of strange fish
look menacingly out of the sky.
You have to come down.
Your dog comes jumping to meet you.
Your island crumbles into the tide of night.

CUANDO TODOS SE VAYAN

Cuando todos se vayan a otros planetas
yo quedaré en la ciudad abandonada
bebiendo un último vaso de cerveza,
y luego volveré al pueblo donde siempre regreso
como el borracho a la taberna
y el niño a cabalgar
en el balancín roto.
Y en el pueblo no tendré nada qué hacer,
sino echarme luciérnagas a los bolsillos
o caminar a orillas de rieles oxidados
o sentarme en el roído mostrador de un almacén
para hablar con antiguos compañeros de escuela.

Como una araña que recorre
los mismos silos de su red
caminaré sin prisa por las calles
invadidas de malezas
mirando los palomares
que se vienen abajo,
hasta llegar a mi casa
donde me encerraré a escuchar
discos de un cantante de 1930
sin cuidarme jamás de mirar
los caminos infinitos
trazados por los cohetes en el espacio.

WHEN EVERYONE GOES

When everyone goes to other planets
I will stay in the abandoned city
drinking a last glass of beer,
and later go back to the town I always go back to
like the drunk to the tavern
and the child to mount the horse
on the broken tongue.
And in the town I will have nothing to do,
except to put fireflies into sacks
or walk the rusted rails
or sit on the gnawed counters of stores
to talk with old classmates.

Like the spider that runs along
the same thread of its web
I will walk unhurried through the streets
invaded by underbrush
looking at the flocks of pigeons
coming down,
until I reach my house
where I will shut myself up
to listen to records of 1930 songs
Never caring to look
at the infinite roads
traced by rockets in space.

SEÑALES

Atardece en el pueblo. Se disuelven
las lejanas humaredas de los cerros.
Los gorriones picotean cerezas pasadas.
El tren de carga pasa
dejando una estela de carbón y mugidos.

"Si llueve con creciente va a llover siete dias," dicen.
Y mientras se alargan sin esperanzas los rieles
el tiempo se despoja de la máscara del verano
y muestra su rostro secreto en la lluvia.

En la trastienda del almacén alzan sus vasos
de pipeño los amigos que ya no nos rescuerdan. El forastero en la
    plazuela
oye contar estrellas a los hijos del carpintero. Y luego
una ronda: "Alicia va en la coche, carolín . . ."

El pueblo se refugia en los ojos de ovejas que dormitan.
Antes de irse, el sol ilumina brutalmente
nuestro rostro condenado al fracaso. Nuestro rostro
y los rostros que nunca conocerán la verdadera realidad

dispersándose como el polvillo de los duraznos
en los dedos del viento: jinetes perdidos, novias
que aún esperan en la capilla ruinosa, vagabundos
con la cabeza destrozada por las locomotoras.

Hasta que el sueño hace señas con su linterna oxidada.
El ángel de la guarda ya no espera nuestro llamado.
Y vemos sin temor que se abre para nosotros
el pais de la noche sin fronteras.

SIGNALS

Dusk falls over the town.
The distant smoke from the hills fades away.
The sparrows are pecking at the withered cherries.
The freight train passes
leaving a wake of a low wail and cinders . . .

"If it rains with a crescent moon," they say,
"It'll rain seven days."
And while the rails, waiting for nothing,
stretch themselves out,
the season sloughs off the mask of summer
and shows its secret face in the rain.

In the back room of the shop
friends who don't remember us raise their glasses.
In the square the stranger listens:
the sons of the carpenter have their fortunes told.
And later, a round:
"Alicia va en el coche, carolin . . ."

The town falls back
into the eyes of half-sleeping sheep.
The sun before it goes
brightens brutally our hopeless face;
our face and the faces never
to know reality

scattering like the powder of peaches
in the wind's fingers:
lost riders, brides that still wait
in the ruined chapel,
tramps with their heads crushed
by locomotives.

DESPEDIDA

Me despido de mi mano
que pudo mostrar el paso del rayo
o la quietud de las piedras
bajo las nieves de antaño.

Para que vuelvan a ser bosques y arenas
me despido del papel blanco y de la tinta azul
de donde surgían ríos perezosos,
cerdos en las calles, molinos vacíos.

Me despido de los amigos
en quines más he confiado:
los conejos y las polillas,
las nubes harapientas del verano,
mi sombra que solía hablarme en voz baja.

Me despido de las virtudes y de las gracias del planeta:
los fracasados, las cajas de música,
los murciélages que al atardecer se deshojan
de los bosques de casas de madera.

Me despido de los amigos silenciosos
a los que sólo les importa saber
dónde se puede beber algo de vino
y para los cuales todos los días
no son sino un pretexto
para entonar canciones pasadas de moda.

Me despido de una muchacha
que sin preguntarme si la amaba o no la amaba
caminó conmigo y se acostó conmigo
cualquíera tarde de esas en que las calles se llenan
de humaredas de hojas quemándose en las acequias.

. . . until the dream sends signals with its rusty lantern.
The guardian angel isn't waiting for our call.
The nation of the night
that has no boundaries
opens itself to us
and we look without fear.

RENUNCIATION

I say goodbye to my hand
that could trace the path of lightning
or wait with a quietness like the stones
that have lain for years under the snow.

So they can go back to be forest and sand
I say goodbye to the paper and ink
from which have risen slow rivers,
pigs in the streets, empty mills.

I say goodbye to the friends
I have trusted most:
the rabbits and the moths,
the ragged clouds of summer,
my shadow that used to speak to me in whispers.

I say goodbye to the virtues and the graces of the planet:
the failures, the music boxes,
the bats that in the evening fly like leaves
from the forests of wooden houses.

I say goodbye to the silent friends
for whom the only important thing is knowing
where a man can get a glass of wine;
for whom the days are flimsy reasons
to sing old songs.

Me despido de una muchacha
cuya cara suelo ver en sueños
iluminada por le triste mirada de linternas
de trenes que parten bajo la lluvia.

Me despido de la memoria
y me despido de la nostalgia
— la sal y el agua
de mis dias sin objeto —

y me despido de estos poemas:
palabras, palabras — un poco de aire
movido por los labios — palabras
para ocultar quizás lo único verdadero:
que respiramos y dejamos respirar.

UN ARBOL ME DESPIERTA

Un árbol me despierta
y me dice: "Es mejor despertar.
Los sueños no te pertenecen.
Mira los gansos que abren
sus grandes alas blancas,
mira los nidales de las gallinas
bajo el automóvil abandonado."

I say goodbye to a girl
who without asking if I loved her
walked with me and went to bed with me
any of those evenings when the streets were filling
with smoke from leaves burning in the gutters.
I say goodbye to a girl
whose face I see in dreams
illuminated by the sad glance
from the lights of trains
starting in the rain.

I say goodbye to memory
and I say goodbye to nostalgia
— the salt and the water
of my meaningless days —

and I say goodbye to these poems:
words, words — a little air moved by the lips —
words to hide perhaps the only truth:
that we breathe and leave off breathing.

A TREE WAKES ME UP

A tree wakes me up
and says to me: It's better to wake up.
Dreams have nothing to do with you.
Look at the geese opening their
great white wings,
look how the chickens have built their nests
under the abandoned car.

ARMANDO URIBE ARCE

Translated by
MILLER WILLIAMS

Armando Uribe Arce, born in 1934, is the
author of two volumes of poetry and a critical
book on Ezra Pound. Easily the least rhetorical
of Chile's poets, he writes a verse that con-
sistently invites comparison with the haiku, not
only in its form and length, but in the strangely
oriental attitude and manner of expression.
Recently returned from lecturing and reading
in this country, Uribe practices law in Santiago.

POEMAS

Yo te amo y los rosales
dan rosas. Yo doy pies,
yo doy manos y ojos.

Y los rosales dan rosas.

No sé mi nombre,
podría ser
hueso o gusano.
Vivo en el huerto
bajo el olivo.

¿Quién eres tu?
¿Cómo eres tu?
(son las preguntas que hago
cuando converso con niñas).

Unas me contestan "no sé"
otras me contestan "hasta luego"
pero las más amadas
callan y suspiran
como si yo fuera ellas.

POEMS

I love you and the rosebush
gives roses. I give feet,
I give hands and eyes.

And the rosebush gives roses.

*   *   *

I don't know my name,
it could be
bone or maggot.
I live in the orchard
under the olive tree.

*   *   *

Who are you?
What are you?
(These are the questions I ask
when I talk to girls.)

Some say "I don't know"
and others "Goodbye"
but those most beloved
sigh and are silent
as if I were them.

La lengua hable de sí: dice: la lengua
es un pez en el agua; el pescador
es el silencio.

Es como una enfermedad
como una enfermedad larga y estéril
caminar por la calle sin nada que hacer
si no es caminar por la calle.

A la hora de doce, a las seis de la tarde, en la manana.
Caminar como sonámbulo, larga y estérilmente
ocupado en parecer ocupado
como un hombre de negocios sin negocios y en quiebra.

The tongue talks of itself: it says: the tongue
is a fish in water; the fisherman
is the silence.

* * *

It's like a sickness
like a long and barren sickness
walking the streets with nothing to do
except to walk the streets.

At noon, at six in the evening, in the morning
with the slow and sterile movement of a sleepwalker
occupied with looking occupied
like a businessman with no business and bankrupt.

POLI DÉLANO

Translated by
CARLYN BARAONA

Poli Délano was born in 1936. He teaches
English at the University of Chile, settled down
now from the travels which during recent years
took him to many parts of Europe and Asia as
well as the United States (where he wrote his
thesis on New York life). His works include
Gente Solitaria (short stories, 1962) and *Cua-
drilatero* (novella, 1962). He received the Premio Alerce of the Society of Writers in 1961.
A novel by Délano will appear this year.

THE BOARDING HOUSE

W ITH some difficulty he unbuttoned his coat to reach the keys in his pants' pocket. A gust of cold wind hit his chest. He coughed. Still walking rapidly he took out the keys and buttoned his coat. Once inside the door of the old house, he stood for a while without moving, leaning against the staircase, hesitating before deciding to climb the long stairs leading to the second floor. Why did it always have to be the same? Every day the same long stairway to his room. He raised both hands and pressed them against his chest and breathed deeply two or three times. Damn! How it hurt. His breath escaped with a half sigh and a groan. It was all so sudden! He climbed slowly, step after step, until finally he reached the top. And then the hallway. The dark, narrow hallway, the long line of doors. How far, dear God! Why did it have to be so far! Halfway there he stopped and rubbed his chest, letting his hand drop to his stomach. The pain was becoming sharper. Sweat broke out on his neck and forehead and ran from his armpits. Groaning with the pain, he unbuttoned his coat, took a handkerchief from his vest pocket, and wiped his face. A door in front of him opened reluctantly. The figure of a woman in a robe was framed against the weak yellow light inside, her hair disarranged.

"Oh, it was you . . . I thought . . ."

Don Rafael didn't answer. The poor woman had probably imagined it was her husband. Her husband, who night after night would come lurching and swearing down the narrow hallway, bumping from wall to wall. The door closed and left him again in the deep rectangle of darkness. He went on down the hall. All the rooms were dark. What were the people doing? Where were they? Sleeping? Were they still out in the streets? Why come home? A few blocks away the lights of the city were still bright. Movies and nightclubs. Girls passing, showing their charms and colors. And all within a few blocks. The city was becoming modernized. Santiago had all at once begun to live at night. Not the way it was in his days. He moved slowly past the darkened rooms until he reached the end of the hall, crossed a small archway, turned right, and faced the door of his own room, the darkest, farthest, and smallest room in the boarding house. He lit the small kerosene stove for a little heat. He wouldn't try to eat. The smell of the kerosene seemed to cut into his guts and it was too much for him to fight. His stomach turned over. He managed to drag the pan from under the bed before he emptied himself in vomits and laments. Coughs and complaints. Cries of pain and nausea. God, how it hurt! Don Rafael fell back on the bed.

"Amanda! . . ." He called out with what little voice he had left. "Amanda . . . Amanda! . . ."

Finally a woman appeared in the doorway. He had called her, yes. But it wasn't Amanda. It was Iris.

"Don Rafael." She touched his shoulder, shaking him gently. "What is it? What's the matter?"

Don Rafael opened his eyes. It wasn't Amanda.

"Amanda . . . I mean Iris . . . Quick, a doctor! In my notebook . . ." He gasped for air.

"Why don't you get in bed, Don Rafael?"

". . . In my notebook, Iris, on top of the table . . . Doctor Mora, Iris, hurry please. Mora. Doctor Mora."

The woman found the notebook. "I'll go call him right away, Don Rafael." And she left the room.

He got into bed. What in God's name was the matter with him? To be sick now. As if he didn't have enough problems. To be sick now, in this hovel, alone, poor, but worst of all, alone. Where were all his old friends? And the girls? Had they forgotten him? To be sick now and in this dirty hovel. He remembered that time before when he had gotten sick. But it was different, that little apartment. He was twenty then and had just begun to make a way for himself. He had begun to make money. Rafael Duran. A brown cashmere suit. But the same day he received it he had gotten sick. It was bronchitis that time. And now what the devil was it? His liver? Possibly the liver. But then it was his bronchials. Hello, hello. Amanda . . . it's me. I'm not feeling very good. It looks like I'll have to stay in bed a couple of days. I thought I'd let you know so you could come by. Tell Sylvia to come too . . . and bring something to eat. I'll pay you later . . . End of . . . End of April. It was April then. The middle of autumn. In the park, right in front of his building, the leaves crackled underfoot. He and Amanda liked to make them crackle, running and jumping in them. A light breeze blew. Couples still made love on the park benches. Isn't that right, Amanda? The children played and dogs ran back and forth before the vigilant eyes of well-dressed ladies. April, the last days of April. One or two days off from work wouldn't matter. He would have to stay in bed. It was a small apartment he had been able to furnish with the help of friends. Old, worn-out pieces of furniture. But good enough. Everything had seemed good to him then. One wall covered with pictures. All of them girls. Some he knew well . . . And others, movie actresses. Beautiful women. Pola Negri. He opened his eyes and looked at the wall, now nothing but dust and cobwebs. Pola, you must be old by now if you still live on this earth.

Señor Duran was overcome by another surge of pain and moaning. That girl? Where has she gone that she still hasn't come with the doctor? He became a little calmer. Pola Negri with her enormous eyes . . . One day he had bought a gramophone to keep on the table by his bed. That was when he was beginning to earn money. Money to live. To invite his friends over. Let's go out to eat. Then dancing, the four of us — what do you say? They were always willing. But Gaspar was the most willing of all, the most enthusiastic. Gaspar, with all the records. Gaspar Martinez, lawyer. That's what his calling cards read now. Gaspar of the light eyes. The other day having a coffee in the Café Haiti he seemed old. Gaspar Martinez, lawyer. *Agustinas . . . Agustinas* what number? Or did the card say Moneda? *Moneda* or *Agustinas.* Good old Gaspar, who always showed up with records, borrowed here and there, and brought to the apartment. Three or four days and he'd take them somewhere else and bring others. Songs, waltzes whirling incessantly around the gramophone. Unending waltzes. And tangos.

Padre nuestro que estas en los cielos,
que todo lo sabes, que todo lo ves . . .

What's left of all that music? Where can you hear it? Where, where? I want to listen to it. I want to hear it! Is that girl never coming with the doctor? Where could she have gone to? He grabbed his stomach with both hands and rolled from one side to the other between the dirty sheets, sighing and moaning. It's not bronchitis. What will I do if I have to stay in bed like the other time? I'll have to stay in bed tomorrow, Amanda. But tomorrow had become a month. Almost a month in bed! All kinds of medicines. Well, he had money then. He could stay in bed a month if he wanted. And friends who would come to visit. Girls to take care of him. Amanda to bring his breakfast. Amanda who was usually so lazy about getting up in the morning. And she would leave after lunch when Sylvia came to stay until supper. Isn't that right, Amanda? Sylvia? Isn't that right? And Sylvia, didn't you stay all night once when I was feeling very bad? Poor thing. You went to sleep in the chair Albert gave me. The chair that Albert brought from home because it was stuck away in the garage. Isn't that how it was, Sylvia? Amanda? Albert? A whole month in bed. But on the second day the news had gotten around. Everyone knew that Rafael Duran had fallen sick. And all his friends kept coming, bringing fruit and vegetables, pastries and sausages, filling up his little kitchen with them . . . Why hasn't that girl come back? . . . Good God! Why hasn't the doctor come?

"Doctor . . . A doctor, please . . . A doctor!"

*　　*　　*

"Where are you going, Iris?"

"I'm going to the *emporio*, ma'm, to make a phone call."

"But it's ten o'clock, Iris. Do you think you'll find it open? I'm sure that . . ."

"Then I'll go to the drugstore, ma'm . . . Or some place."

"And why are you in such a hurry?"

"Don Rafael is sick, and he sent me to call a doctor . . . You ought to see how he looks . . . All yellow."

"Well, all right, go on, but first you'll have to take Señor Riveros his supper. He came in late and didn't want to go to the dining room."

"Yes, ma'm. Right away."

Iris stops in front of one of the doors in the long hall. She knocks.

"Come in."

"Good evening, Señor Riveros." He's not so ugly, even if he is on the skinny side. He's not so old either. Not much over forty. It was one of those rooms without a window, dark, with only a faded yellow bulb. Old walls papered who knows how long ago. Atrocious wallpaper, stained and torn. A bronze bed with the head against the wall. Beside it, a writing table with paper scattered across it.

"Good evening, Iris. How very pretty you look . . ."

She glances down at her green skirt and the woolen sweater her mother has sent her for her birthday. It's a nice sweater. She puts the tray on the table.

"I changed clothes. I have to go out."

"Oh, I see . . . Hey, these potatoes aren't bad. And that's why you're all fixed up, is it?"

She nods.

"Come on now. You have a date with someone, don't you?"

Iris laughs and comes closer. Everything seems strange tonight. Maybe it's because of her birthday. He's not bad looking even if he is skinny. He's not so very old. What could have become of Sergio? It's been more than a week since he called. She could stand not seeing him, but she hadn't even had a word of him. He used to send some kid over with a message, but now . . . He's walked out. Probably he's walked out on her . . . like all the rest of them.

"No, it's just that I have to find a telephone . . . Don Rafael isn't feeling good . . ."

"Look, Iris . . . Why don't you sit down for a while . . ."

She looks straight into his eyes. He laughs awkwardly and knows his laugh sounds forced and knows she realizes it too and he feels embarrassed. He takes her arm with an air of gallantry and leads her to the chair beside him.

"Wait till I finish eating. I'm not going to eat any more sausage. Then we'll smoke a cigarette, O.K.? Look, a friend gave me a Pall Mall this afternoon. American . . ."

Iris isn't impressed.

"Wouldn't you like some coffee, Señor Riveros?"

"No. No, I don't care for any coffee . . ."

He puts his hand on her leg. She stands up.

"But some tea, then, huh?"

He takes hold of her arm and with a napkin in the other hand he wipes his mouth.

"No tea either . . . Here, have a cigarette. Come on. Why don't you sit down?"

He laughs. She sits down. His hand drops from her arm to her thigh. With the other hand he takes out his lighter and lights both cigarettes. She coughs. Then she looks at him, asking questions with her eyes. His hands answer her. Two flies land on a piece of sausage. Cigarette smoke fills the room. He kisses her and she lets him. He kisses her and covers her breasts with his hands. Always the kisses first. She lets him. Everything is so strange tonight. Maybe it's because of her birthday. He stands up and pulls her up with him.

"I must go. God, I must go, Señor Riveros. I have to call the doctor . . ."

He holds her and draws her close to him.

"Wait . . . Wait . . ."

He pushes her little by little toward the bed. He turns off the light.

"It's still early. Why the hurry? I'll go with you later."

From the bed comes a small cry.

"Please, Señor Riveros, please, I have to go call . . . Afterwards if you want . . ."

Señor Riveros is not listening.

"Don't worry about it. Later we'll go together. Wherever you say. We'll take a taxi."

* * *

The fuel is almost gone. The flame is dying. The smell of the burnt kerosene is heavy in the room. Señor Duran, lying on his back, hands crossed over his stomach, gasps and then stops fighting. She must have called by now and the doctor is coming. Will be here any moment. She must have called him by now. God knows what it is to have to depend on a servant girl, someone who maybe doesn't care if he is dying or not . . . No, Iris is a good girl. Simple. Affectionate. She has called by now and the doctor is on his way. He's known her for a long time. For years. When he moved into this house she was already here, a young girl then, only sixteen or seventeen, straight from the country, always helpful and pleasant. She must be almost thirty now. But was it Iris? Is this the same one? He'll have to ask her. Were you here when I first came? Or better to ask her if she was here when that fellow killed himself. That's it. That was the first night he had eaten in the boarding house. He had sat down at the table, there was only one table then for all the boarders, and they were waiting for the second course. It was brought in and this fellow stood up and looked at all of us, defiant, desperate. Beans, he shouted, beans again! Almost crying he let go the table edge and walked quickly out the front door. The next morning he was found dead in his room, wrists cut with a razor blade. Months later his act was understandable. For precaution, Elena, the owner of the boarding house, had introduced some variations in the menu. They no longer had beans. Now they had potatoes. Day after day after day. That was the first night. If Iris remembers that fellow, then she is the same girl. He would ask her. The pain has gone away some. To be alone. To get sick and alone. What rotten luck! What old and rotten luck! His good luck that had been with him those first years, had lasted only until he got to Paris. When his ship had sailed, the dock had been full of his friends. Full of flowers and kisses, of tears and promises. Amanda crying down there on the dock. Back on land, Amanda crying while the young man of good fortune left to try his luck in the old world. Why hadn't he stayed home? How different his life would have been. Paris. Poverty. Pure poverty. His best years lost. The false Bohemian life; the hours spent in some café on Montparnasse; trying here and there to earn a living, sometimes in shameful ways when the hunger was too much to bear. He is alone, drinking a pernod in the *Rendez Vous*. Waiting. He is young. Good-looking. His suit is pressed. Finally the bell rings. He lifts the receiver of the phone at his table. *Oui? . . . Bon soir, monsieur . . .* his heart trembles . . . *Est-ce que vous êtes tout seul, monsieur? . . . Moi? . . . Oui, oui, madame . . .* Then months of easy life and days of boredom. Nights of boredom satisfying a worn out, roughened body. But one must live. And life is hard. When there is money one lives well. Young women. The *boulevard . . .* Damn that doctor! Why doesn't he hurry up! Why doesn't he get here? Pain. Collapse. He draws his legs up and groans.

"Hello . . . Can I come in?"

It's the landlady. It's Elena. Señor Duran wants to say "come in" but he only makes a few guttural, incomprehensible sounds. The door opens and closes again. She walks over to the bed. She puts her hand on his forehead and feels for his pulse. How yellow he is! How ghostly. How different from the days when they . . .

"Do you feel any better? The girl said you weren't well . . . Can I get you anything?"

"I'm better, Elena. Don't worry. Iris has gone to call the doctor. He ought to be here soon."

She looks at him with compassion. But there is rancor in his voice. He hasn't forgiven her. She understands that. He will never forgive her. Poor Rafael. But what could she do? Her reputation was first, the name her father had left her. The three years in jail were not much fun, of course. But, merciful God, for years now, ever since he got out, she hadn't charged him a cent for his room and board. It hadn't been easy for her either. A couple of idiots! Trying to take Madame Durandean's jewels! But what a life they could have led if things had worked out. What a life! She looks at him with tenderness. How old he seems! How the time goes for us all. She wanted to cry. Where was her little girl? Not a single card. Nothing. Maybe she didn't even remember. Her own baby! The only thing in this world she cared for. Her eyes, her life, the center of her love. Oh, Rafael, you were guilty too. And I also paid. Don't try to play innocent, don't blame me for it all! She dries the sweat from his forehead and leaves the room.

*   *   *

"Iris, maybe it's better if I don't go with you. I have to get up pretty early tomorrow."

She doesn't answer. She puts on the sweater her mother sent her for her birthday. She doesn't care if Señor Riveros goes with her or not. It is better if he doesn't. Nothing has been right. Not like Sergio was with her. But it was part of her life. It had been for years. Going to bed with the boarders. Nothing unusual about it. Have to please the guests. Doesn't Señora Elena say it all the time? It began with the medical student. The one in the second room to the right, the one Señora Elena's daughter was in love with. He came home one morning when she was scrubbing the floor. Both of them in the room and it was easy for him. And every night after that. The only thing was that Señora Elena couldn't find out. Then the truck driver. And then that dirty pig of a public official. And now this skinny Riveros. He would want her again tomorrow. One night was never enough for any of them. But none of them was like Sergio. Sergio who had whispered such nice things to her. Who watched the twilight with her from the top of the hill. Sergio, from whom she hadn't heard for over a week. Sergio, who had taken her dancing so many times at the *quinta*. With him it had been different. Everything had happened without thinking. Without planning. Maybe it was because she hadn't heard from him that she was here now with this skinny Señor Riveros. And maybe if she had seen him or he had sent her a message by some kid, she would be here just the same. Anyway, it was best to go by herself to phone. She walks over to the door. He holds her back a moment.

"Here, take this . . . you can take a taxi."

Without answering, she leaves the room, crosses the hall with an absent look on her face, and goes down the long stairs to the street. The air outside brings her to life. She shivers. Then she opens her fist and looks at what Señor Riveros has put there. *Three escudos.* Three *escudos* to take a taxi . . . bitterness seizes her. She is unconscious of her movements until, in the middle of some street, two buses roaring by like green monsters make her jump. Where will she find a public telephone at this hour? Jesus! Where will she ever find one at this hour!

* * *

And Amanda and Sylvia and Gaspar and Albert, why don't they come? Everybody, why don't they come? Why don't they bring food? And the records. A little music, please, play some music. Something good to dance to. Would you like to dance, señorita? That's how he had met her — at a school dance. Amanda studied pharmacy. They had gone out together often. She got to know his friends—Sylvia, Gaspar, and the rest. And the good years together. She liked him, liked him a lot. You loved me, Amanda, didn't you? Rafael Duran was a fortunate young man. But he wasn't meant for marriage; he didn't want to be tied down. Not before he'd had the best of the green years. And you had the best didn't you, Rafael? Look what's become of you. You got the best of the green years, didn't you? Hungry in Paris. Begging the consul to send you back home. What dignity! Coming back with half the life you had when you left. Then seeing your name in all the Santiago papers:

"Three years for jewel thief."

Rotting away in a cell. And afterwards unable to work. No will.

Begging a little blackmail to get a filthy room and a mouthful of food. Your hair gray and your skin full of wrinkles. You weren't the kind to marry, Rafael Duran. You had to get the best out of the green years. But get married now, Rafael, get married now. What are you waiting for? Amanda, why didn't I marry you? Amanda? You loved me. You cared for me. Didn't you, Amanda? They all did. Everyone liked Rafael. How were you, Amanda? How was your face? Did you look like Pola Negri? I can't remember, Amanda. Amanda, I can't remember what you looked like. Good God! What time is it? Where is the doctor? The pains. He turns to one side. The bedclothes in a pile. The pain growing more intense. It's the ulcer. The doctor told you. He warned you one day the drinking would finish you off. A little drink every so often, what harm could it do? A little drink everyday, what harm could it do? A few drinks everyday, what harm could it do? Ay, ay! God! It's the ulcer, it's the ulcer.

"Amanda, Amanda, bring the doctor, hurry, the doctor."

The cry barely reaches the walls. Señor Duran manages to sit up a little and tries to call out.

* * *

Downtown the green and red and purple lights turn off and on neurotically. Iris is in a bar, the only place she could find a telephone. Doctor Mora has gone out to eat with his fiancée. She dials the fiancée's number. He has just left, ten minutes ago. He will be back soon. She orders a beer. Then calls again. No, not yet. She orders another beer, she dials again: "Yes, yes, Señor Rafael Duran wants you to come. He is very ill . . . Who? . . . Señor Rafael Duran . . . Rafael Duran, Rafael Duran, ah yes! Tell him right away . . ." She walks back towards the boarding house. A wind blows. To chill the bones. Two men cross in front of her, say something to her. She doesn't bother to look at them. She laughs. Ja! She has had two beers. When had she drunk two beers before, unless it was with Sergio? For a moment she wants to cry. But what about, what for? Wasn't it the same with all the boarders? It all began with the young medical student. The one who was soft on the landlady's daughter. Then that pig of a public official and the truck driver. Why cry? It wouldn't be any different if she were to learn Sergio hadn't walked out on her. All of them wanted her, all of them at the boarding house wanted her. This time the skinny one. Tomorrow, God knows who. It would always be like that if Sergio didn't come back. It was the same with all the boarders . . . A few years back even Don Rafael himself. . . .

*　*　*

The scream pierces her hearing like a sharp needle, even though his room is far away. She listens. They all listen. Some of them look out their doors into the hall. What happened? What in the hell is going on? She puts on her robe and slippers and walks toward the sick man's room. She turns in without knocking. The bedclothes are on the floor. The bedpan is turned over. Don Rafael is lying with his eyes closed. He is peaceful. She becomes frightened. She goes to his side.

"Rafael . . . Rafael!" She takes hold of his hand.

He opens, half opens, his eyes and presses her hand to his chest. He tries to smile.

"Amanda, you've come . . . You're just like Pola Negri, Amanda. It was April, the middle of autumn. You care for me, don't you, Amanda? Don't you? It was autumn and remember how we used to jump in the leaves . . . ?"

His mouth stays open. But his eyes have closed. Tears, the tears of a woman, fall on his stiffened, unfeeling fingers. It is Amanda or Elena crying over the dried leaves trampled in autumn.

ANTONIO SKARMETA

Translated by
CECLIA BOISIER

Antonio Skarmeta, born in 1940, has published
short stories in various magazines and anthologies, written a musical comedy which was produced last year, and has translated into Spanish
works of Albee and Saroyan. Among the liter-
ary awards which have come to him are one for
the musical, one in the important Concurso
Crav for 1964, and the short story award in
the Concurso Literarie Arte y Universidad for
the story which is included here.

FIRST COMES THE SEA

"FIRST comes the sea," my cousin said. "And then the sun, and then the night. If that's what you wanted to know, you're dismissed. Hand me the hammer."

I reached under the fender and found it. I handed it to him quickly. He grabbed it and started to hammer a pipe with brief, violent blows; it might have been the exhaust pipe; I know nothing about automobiles.

"It has to be straightened out," he said, hammering away.

"That's not what I wanted to know," I said.

"What did you want to know?"

"Well . . . about the sea and the sun and then the wind."

"No, not the wind. After the sun, the night."

"All right," I said. "It was not that."

"Let's see," my cousin said.

"You were studying Literature."

"O.K. Go on."

"You were Angelica's guy."

"What's that? I couldn't hear you."

"You aren't going to hear me if you keep beating on that damn pipe!"

Without stopping, he turned around for a second and glanced at me. Then he looked back at the pipe, turned it over, and started to hammer on the other side.

"You're not very polite," I said.

"If you think the sea doesn't come first, all right."

"I don't know," I said.

"Talked to my father, didn't you?"

"Yes."

"I can see why he's worried all right, but not you!"

"I want to know," I said.

He stopped hammering, looked at the sky and blinked. He looked over the car, walking around it, took me by the shoulder, and without a word we went over to sit on the grass.

"You're the best of the family," he said to me.

"Oh, come on!"

"I mean it. You're going to be somebody."

"Your father's also somebody," I said. "You are too."

"Not yet. Papa's somebody in a certain way. He's got money."

"Besides, he worries about you."

"I don't like that," he said.

"He wants you to finish your studies. And I think he's right," I said. "I think he's damn right, if you want to know."

He jumped up. He went in the kitchen through the back door, then after a while he kicked the door open and came out with drinks in his hands. He sat down beside me and handed me one.

"What were you saying?"

"I think he's damn right," I said.

"No. Before that."

"You were Angelica's guy," I answered.

"I agree."

"I like her, I really do. I like her being your girl."

"We'll pick her up when I finish with the car," he said.

"She coming with us?"

"I promised her," he said.

Then he added: "College is not right. A guy like me's got nothing to do in college."

He leaned back against the apple tree.

"What do you want?" I said to him. "You've got money, good grades, you had Angelica. What do you want?"

He stretched his arms out, pursed his lips and then shrugged his shoulders.

"To understand," he said.

"Understand what?"

"Everything. I'm a fool."

"You're the smartest one in the family," I said. "You're no fool. Why should you quit school? Nobody has grades as good as yours. What's the matter with you?"

He downed his drink and rolled the bottle across the grass till it stopped against my shoe.

"Let's finish the car," he said. "Otherwise there won't be any sun left at the beach."

But he stayed there against the tree, with no apparent intention of going on with the work. I got up and put some tools in the box.

"Things happen to you sometimes," he said.

"Like what?"

"I don't know. Things."

"Don't know what you're talking about," I said. "Let's finish the job."

He walked toward the car, opened the door, and started the engine. Then he leaned against the wheel, looked in the distance, and ran his hand over the windshield.

"I like to feel free," he said. "To feel my hands at work, touch my naked body, to talk. I like my woman to be free. I like to lie down with my woman freely and talk. You understand?"

"You should be a writer," I said.

"I will be."

Then he leaned back and breathed deeply.

"The best one," he said. "There are things that happen to you. You think I sound dramatic?"

"Yes."

"Does it bother you?"

"No," I said. "I like it. I know you well."

"You're the best of the family," he said again. "Even though you haven't been to college."

"I don't go with college."

He stretched out his hand, wrinkled his face, and touched his finger to his chest.

"Me either," he said.

"Yes you do."

"You're always right," he said. "Things happen, you know."

"Right. What shall I tell your old man?"

"Nothing," he said. "Bring the bathing suits and let's go."

"Let's finish the car," I said.

"It's ready. I put the pipe back on and off we go."

I turned to leave but when I opened the front door he stopped me with a whistle.

"The car, for instance," he said. "Did you know that it hasn't been running for three months?"

He looked at me, then raised his eyebrows and lifted up his head as if he were consulting me.

"O.K.?"

"O.K.," I said. "And want to know something else?"

"What?"

"If you start writing you're gonna be the best. Want to know why?"

"Go on."

" 'Cause you don't make a braggy fuss about anything."

"All right," he said. "That's not enough. At college we study writers who brag."

"It's different. You want to understand," I said.

"That's not enough either."

"O.K., you are dramatic, dammit!"

"O.K.," he said. "You're the best of the family. Go get the bathing suits."

I went in and ran upstairs; in my cousin's room I found the bathing suits, two towels, and a pack of cigarettes and put them in the bag. I was about to run down when I met my uncle coming out of his room.

"How's it going?" he said. "What's he doing now?"

"He fixed the car," I said. "We're going to the beach."

"So he fixed the car, how 'bout that! He's a smart kid. And about school, what does he say?"

"Nothing."

"Nothing?"

"Don't worry," I said. "We're in a hurry."

"I have to worry. He's my son."

"He'll go on studying. If you want to know, he can't live without studying."

"How do you know?"

"Sometimes these things happen," I said. And ran downstairs.

We got in and started off, at full speed. The car ran smoothly, easily. It had never sounded so good before, but my cousin didn't boast about it. After a while, about noon, we stopped in front of Angelica's house and my cousin went for her. I got out too, went into the coffee shop on the corner, and phoned the office that I wouldn't be at work that afternoon because I was sick. Then I asked for a Coke, started a record in the Wurlitzer, and lit a cigarette.

When I got back to the car I noticed my cousin's face had changed. His lips were pursed and he was frowning. Sitting beside him, Angelica greeted me with a slight smile as I sat down on her right, put my elbow on the window, and kept silent. After a while we turned onto the highway to the coast, and later we passed the airport, and then went through the town of Melipilla. My cousin was driving at full speed and hadn't said a word. Angelica and I looked at the landscape and smoked.

When we got to Cartagena beach, he slowed down along the coast road, looking at the people, and the hills, and the sea. Then he gained speed again and didn't stop until we got to Las Cruces beach.

"This will do," he said. "You like it?"

"Sure."

"How about you?" he asked Angelica.

"I like it very much."

We undressed in the car, put our suits on, and walking slowly went over to stretch out on the sand near the water.

My cousin lay on his stomach, stretched his arms and scooped up fistfuls of sand, which he pressed tight and let fall slowly.

Angelica lay on her back and I remained sitting, smoking and watching her brown, slim body, and her black hair shining against the sand. She was just as I had met her a year before, when my cousin took me along and introduced her to me and told me she was it, that she was scatterbrained, but she was it anyway. Now she had changed; my cousin had been creating her, filling her life with his strength and wisdom.

"What's the matter?" I said.

"He got that way," she said. "All of a sudden."

"What?"

"I don't know. What does he want? I've been all right," she said. "What does he want?"

"To understand."

She got up, took a cigarette and I lit it for her.

"I'll never really know him. He's different," she said.

"Yeah. He's different."

"What do you think?" she said.

"Everything'll be fine."

Later on my cousin got up, took Angelica by the arm and they walked toward the sea. Just before they reached the water, they stopped and talked for a few minutes. Then they went in, beyond their depth, and kept swimming for a while. I lit a cigarette and smoked it slowly, looking at the sky with the sun in my eyes. The day was clear, no wind, some birds singing above.

Angelica ran up to me, dried her face and her body, sat down on the towel, fixed her hair, and smiled.

"Everything's fine," she said.

"Good," I said. "What's he doing now?"

"He's floating. He likes to lie on his back and float."

"He's going to be a writer," I said.

We kept talking for an hour or more and my cousin went on floating, and sometimes swimming, and sometimes diving from a rock. Then I went into the water, swam up to him, and we had a race, which I won. We sat on a rock and my cousin, breathless, nodded toward Angelica on the beach.

"She," he said.

"O.K.," I said.

"O.K."

* * *

Night was coming when we started back. They sat in back and

I drove to Santiago with the windows open and the warm November wind blowing hard against my face. We took Angelica home, and when we got to our house we went into the kitchen, put some cheese between pieces of bread, and bit into them. Then we went up to the room. My cousin sat at his desk, took out two books and some sheets of paper.

"The sea was O.K.," he said.

"Right."

"For me, it's the most important thing."

Then he handed me one of the books.

"Latin," he said.

Then he passed me the other one.

"Classic Spanish. Cervantes."

"Lope de Vega," I said.

"The Arcipreste de Hita."

"La Vida es Sueño," I said. I took off my shoe and threw it at him.

"Magnificent books," he said.

Then he turned in the seat, leaned his elbows on the table, put his head in his hands, and began to study. I opened *Don Quixote* at chapter thirty-three, lay on the bed, and didn't stop reading till three in the morning. Then I put the book on the floor, covered my face with the pillow, and fell asleep. As far as I know, my cousin went on studying.

RAÚL RUÍZ

Translated by
MILLER WILLIAMS

Raúl Ruíz was born in 1942. The son of a ship captain, he has studied philosophy and mathematics and is busy directing for radio, television, and the movies when he is not writing or reading. Since the first production of his work, when he was sixteen, Ruíz has been one of Chile's boldest and most energetic young playwrights.

THE CHEATER

By RAÚL RUÎZ

Translated by MILLER WILLIAMS

CHARACTERS

A WIDOW, of fifty or sixty years

A COLONEL, perhaps a little older

A YOUNG MAN

A room in an old house. Almost all the furniture is covered with sheets. The only pieces visible are a couch, a table, a chair, a gramaphone. A male store-window dummy in an old army uniform stands at attention. The walls have been decorated with a pair of recruiting posters from the First World War, plus a couple of old carbines, swords, daggers. The entire theatre has been lightly sprayed with Wizard brand home deodorizer (for bathroom).

The widow is sitting upstage center, facing the audience. She contorts her face into various shapes, and begins applying rouge to her cheeks. With an obvious impatience she covers her face with powder, and a small cloud rises. She accentuates the lines of her face with an eyebrow pencil: enormous bags under the eyes, sunken cheeks, off-color eyebrows. When she stops bothering with her face, neither the nose nor the mouth are where they should be, and the eyes have grown. There has been a steady crescendo in lights and action.

The widow closes her eyes, smiles, shakes her head.

There is a knock at the door. The widow starts. Another knock. She gets to her feet and hesitates. A third knock, and she moves reluctantly toward the door. As she passes in front of the couch, she lifts from it an enormous red wig, fluffs it and puts it on.

More knocking. She moves uncertainly, finally answers with two knocks of her own.

From the other side come two more knocks, sounding very hollow.
The widow gives several short knocks. Two come back.

VOICE: Good afternoon. (*Two knocks*) Today is Monday.
WIDOW: Monday?
VOICE: Yes, Madam. Good afternoon.
Pause. The widow opens the door, and the head of the colonel
pokes abruptly into the room. He is made-up for a silent movie,
much like that of the widow. Under his arm is a briefcase.
COL: Am I late?
WID: No.
He enters the room, studies it as if he had never been there before.
COL: A nice place. You're doing all right as a widow.
WID: I manage.
COL: May I sit down? (*He indicates the couch*)
WID: Not there.
COL: Oh. I beg your pardon. (*Remains standing*)
WID: Cognac or vodka?
COL: Yes. Mix them up together. (*Pauses*) A nice place. (*Takes*
the drink) Thanks. And you?
WID: No.
COL: (*Stroking her face*) Still in mourning?
WID: Sit down.
COL: (*Sits on the forbidden couch*) Ah, the years pass! May I take
off my shoes?
The widow doesn't answer. The colonel removes his shoes and scoots
them under the couch, from where he takes a pair of slippers which
he puts on. He lets out a long sigh.
COL: A very nice place. You're doing very well as a widow.
WID: Let's get to the subject.
They look at each other and smile as if they were partners in a
conspiracy.
COL: Did you get my letter?
WID: Many letters.
COL: What did you think of the last one?

WID: I don't believe you.

COL: My dear lady, you've got to believe me.

WID: Persuade me. My mind is not closed.

COL: My first words will convince you.

WID: Go ahead.

COL: (*Clearing his throat*) I'll be brief: (*Assumes a rhetorical air*) "Your late husband, present here. . . ." (*Indicates the dummy*)

WID: You are not to mention him.

COL: Or better yet: "Around town they are saying . . . there is some discussion. . . ."

WID: Go on. . . .

COL: ". . . with respect to your fortune."

The widow chuckles suddenly. Silence.

COL: That is not my point, Madam.

WID: Money. Are you short of cash?

COL: Yes. My friends and I are . . . have been thinking . . . that if you were to pass on to a better life. . . .

The widow takes the briefcase and turns her back on the colonel.

WID: With your permission. . . .

COL: If you were to suffer an accident, perhaps. . . .

WID: (*Looking into the briefcase*) Something new? (*She puts a hand into the briefcase and pulls out a shoe, two handkerchiefs, some stones, a belt, a bloody military cap. With these she completes the uniform of the dummy.*)

COL: (*Painfully*) . . . and the door were to remain open . . .

WID: (*Her back still to the colonel*) Go on. . . .

COL: I was saying that my friends and I. . . .

WID: What friends? You said that already!

COL: (*Resigned to the futility of the conversation, pulls a hatchet from inside his jacket, approaches the widow slowly*) A professor of history, a druggist, a distant cousin . . . some other people. They thought we might try to. . . .

WID: Say that again?

COL: (*Louder*) They thought that if you and I agreed, and if I. . . . (*He lifts the hatchet*)

WID: What!?

COL: That if you closed your eyes. . . . (*He swings the blade to decapitate her, but she moves casually out of his reach. He decapitates the dummy instead. She turns and looks at him impassively.*)

COL: (*Disheartened*) I failed!

WID: (*Irritated*) Yes.

COL: Just one more chance! I promise to land it right!

WID: (*Softly*) You don't have to be in such a hurry.

COL: But you're not cooperating. You keep moving around. (*He serves himself another glass of cognac and vodka*) I have to plan all the details without you.

WID: (*Screwing the head back on the dummy*) Help me with this thing. . . .

COL: I'm not bringing it off.

WID: Hand me the hat.

The colonel hands it to her, getting his hands stained with blood. He wipes them on his clothes.

WID: The blood is real? That is to say . . . is it . . . is it the right . . . age?

COL: Almost. Have you noticed the belt?

WID: Fresh. . . .

COL: That blood will not dry, Madam. He was a hero.

WID: You're a damned liar!

COL: Now, you don't want to provoke me!

WID: You ought not to be here.

COL: I beg your pardon!

WID: Must you come here and profane this place?

COL: You, Madam, are an ingrate. Who has reconstructed, in all humility, the hero's image? Who has paid the bills? Who has hunted through heaven and earth for the remains? This hat, fifty yards from the scene of the catastrophe; the jacket, practically pulverized, reconstructed by the best seamstresses available. And this sword . . . what a hell of a mess! And the pants, nothing but the ashes of his underwear. You forget,

Madam. You forget very quickly. I don't even want to talk about the rest, that perfect jewel of an artificial arm, flying to who knows where, finally uncovered by *me*! I won't even mention the complete collection of teeth . . . Madam! (*He is almost screaming*) Are you not going to cry!?

WID: No. I can't . . . (*makes a vague gesture*) The emotion, it won't come. . . .

COL: Make an effort, concentrate. . . .

WID: It's no use.

COL: If you like, I can say it again.

WID: What for?

Pause.

COL: (*Almost inaudibly*) Slap me, then.

The widow gives him a hard slap.

COL: Again!

She slaps him a second time.

COL: Again, again, again againagain (*accelerating, then suddenly . . .*) Enou-u-ugh! (*Closes his eyes, smiles*) Now get away from me. I can feel myself going mad. My legs are tingling. Try to get away from me. Everything is red (*Screaming now*) A military march! (*The widow puts on a record. Marching music*) Perfect, my dear lady. Perfect. Now let me show you the other side of the coin. We are not going to talk about your husband. I don't even know your husband. I heard about his death on the radio. What do you think of that?! (*The widow has an attack of coughing*) Please don't interrupt. I have to concentrate. (*More coughing*) Stop doing that! I have to steal your. . . . (*Coughing*) Don't take that attitude! I'm trying to stay on the subject. Which is not your husband. He was only a pretext. You have money. (*Puts out his hand*) Let me have it. It gives me great pain, Madam, but I intend to leave you without a cent. (*The widow stares at him a moment, then the cough comes back. The colonel takes her by the shoulders and shakes her*) Please. Don't you see, I have to kill you. We can't waste any more time. The neighbors must have heard the screaming. It's now or never. (*He picks up a pair of scissors*) Well, say something. (*She looks at the scissors and screams. The colonel lets them fall automatically*) Did I frighten you?

WID: (*She is panting and smiles at him*) I don't know. (*She strokes his face with great tenderness*) You are very persevering.

COL: Shall we try again?

WID: If you like. (*She sits down. The colonel starts to sit also*) Don't sit there. You'll profane it.

COL: I'll stand.

Pause. Sighs.

WID: Who's going to talk?

COL: You first. I don't have the energy. (*He takes a drink from his glass*)

WID: Sit down.

COL: Thank you. (*Sits again on the forbidden couch*) A very nice apartment. You're doing well as a widow.

WID: Let's make it short. You didn't come here to say that. Are you paying me a social call? No. You were just passing by? No. Did you come to bring me a message? (*Pause*) Say something!

COL: No, Madam. I have come for something else.

Pause. They stare at each other impatiently.

WID: (*Softly.*) I'm sure you haven't come to talk about my husband.

COL: It isn't necessary. (*He closes his hands on her throat, turns his head away.*) Does it hurt?

WID: A little.

COL: (*Continuing to strangle her*) You're taking it too matter-of-factly.

WID: I'm used to it. (*The colonel releases her.*) What's the matter?

COL: I need music.

The widow puts on an opera.

WID: Are you sure you wouldn't prefer a gun?

COL: The powder upsets my stomach. (*Smiles*) Reminds me of the war.

WID: Cognac?

COL: Madam, you are very understanding.

Pause.

WID: I'm waiting.

COL: I have to tie you up. I've always dreamed of it that way.

WID: Do what you want to do.

COL: (*Tying her to a chair*) Be still. I don't like it when you move. I don't want you to look at me. (*He blindfolds her.*)

WID: Are we going to do something degrading?

COL: I'll try. I'm not going to promise.

WID: Talk to me. I'm bored.

COL: Is it important to talk about your husband? For your information I dream about the hero every night. He gives me messages for you. Unfortunately I always forget them. I tell you, I go crazy with those messages. It's a pity, Madam, but I'm the only hope for your husband. I'm the only authorized witness. . . .

WID: You wouldn't know a war if you swallowed one.

COL: Why do you say that?

WID: You've never been outside your house.

COL: That's enough!

WID: Where did you read about my husband's death? In what paper?

COL: Well, I don't read. . . .

WID: And now you're looking for a part of the widow's pension.

COL: (*Laughs*) No, Madam. I have much more noble ambitions.

He finishes tying her up, then runs around the room on tip-toe, looks desperately under the sheets, uncovering other couches and other dummies.

WID: You're making a mess.

COL: I can't help it. I've got to find the treasure.

WID: What treasure?

COL: The jewels, Madam. I'm interested in the jewels. Can't you look at this from my point of view?

WID: You're in a hurry?

COL: If you want to live, split the treasure with me. I mean the jewels.

WID: Gems.

COL: For the last time, while I'm in a generous mood.

WID: You can drop that.

COL: I'm going to torture you.

WID: With what?

COL: Don't ask questions. I have the floor now. For years, Madam, I have heard talk of your treasure. An incalculable fortune. It is right here, only a few yards away. Everybody knows it.

WID: Rumors.

COL: Madam, I am going to torture you.

She escapes from the bonds with no difficulty and pulls off the blindfold.

WID: Kill me.

COL: Everything in good time.

He sinks into a chair.

WID: You've lost your enthusiasm?

COL: I have a cramp in my leg. (*Pause*) Don't look at me like that.

WID: Come over here. . . .

COL: (*Whines*) What am I doing here? They're waiting for me at home. I'll be late. That's your fault . . . you didn't have to invite me!

WID: Come over here. . . .

COL: What good am I going to get out of all this? Tell me, what good? You got me mixed up in it. Gold has been devaluated.

WID: Don't be bashful. . . .

COL: I'm a brave man, Madam. I was brave. I could have made the leap. You've broken me. I don't know how. You got me too involved. It hurts me to say this . . . you've made me lose my head.

WID: Let's don't go off on a tangent.

COL: Don't fool around with me, Madam. I am quite capable of anything.

WID: For instance?

COL: You took us off on it. (*The cramp returns*) Aye-yiiieeeee!

WID: (*Tenderly*) You can't move a finger, can you?

COL: Don't mix me up.

WID: Come over here. . . .

COL: (*Standing dizzily*) I came to kill you.

WID: When did you last see blood?

COL: Oh, I have a number of murders under my belt.

WID: Come over here. . . .

COL: (*Hysterically*) Do you want to lose a finger?

WID: Cut my head off.

COL: (*Coughs, drinks*) You get the best part. You can rest. You will be remembered. They will surround you with candles . . . think of it! You will endure for centuries. You will be canonized. I'm certain of that! And I, on the other hand . . . here as you see me . . . I am a working man. I am a shadow. You have squeezed the juice out of me. Madam, you are a harpy! You have caused me to lose the best years of my life.

WID: Don't put me on a pedestal.

COL: I throw myself on your mercy. I'll never forget. I am a true martyr. Spit on me. Please!

She spits on him. He stifles a scream. She spits on him again. He lets out an almost feminine squeak.

WID: What's the matter?

COL: (*Surprised*) I'm getting mad. (*Feels over his body as if some part might be missing.*) One never stops getting acquainted with himself.

WID: This is the moment. Let's not lose it.

COL: My legs are tingling. That's an unmistakeable sign.

He takes a couple of steps toward the widow. She backs away. He moves slowly after her.

WID: Don't give up.

COL: I'm not going to.

WID: Come on. Come on. . . .

COL: Don't blame me for what happens.

He takes her by the arms, almost faints, falls to his knees and starts to cry.

WID: (*Mussing his hair*) Some day I'll be afraid of you.

COL: (*Still crying*) Kill yourself!

WID: And you. What are you going to do?

COL: It's easy to die. It's very easy. (*He takes a pirate's pistol from the wall and hands it to her.*) Shoot yourself.

WID: You shoot me.

COL: I can't. There are too many things in the way. I'm not young. I've come to like you. I keep thinking about your husband . . . I had to meet him . . . and my debts. My hands are tied. On the other hand, you . . . what do you have to live for? You are free, completely free. You are already dead. Just make the effort. Give me what you have and kill yourself. Now! Do it now!

WID: No. You mustn't insist.

COL: There are other ways. It wouldn't be any trouble, for instance, to go over to the window. (*He opens the window, lets in the noise from outside.*) Think about the clean, fresh air. Think about the vertigo. It's an uncommon pleasure. Now you have it. Open your arms. A little will-power and you're lost. . . .

WID: And you go right on, without suffering anything.

COL: I promise you, I guarantee you I will punish myself. I only ask you to do this first. I just want to see you fall, and then after a while to dream of you in the other world.

WID: Help me. . . .

COL: No.

They look at each other without moving.

WID: It's getting dark.

COL: I have to go. I live a long way from here.

WID: Will you come to see me again?

COL: Next Monday. (*Looks at his watch.*) We still have five minutes. Put on the last waltz.

She puts on a record. She pours two glasses of cognac and both of them drink.

WID: Cheers.

COL: Cheers. Shall we dance?

They begin dancing, moving heavily back and forth between the pieces of furniture. Their silhouettes are barely visible.

WID: We could be taken for husband and wife.

COL: If we had met before. . . .

WID: (*Laughs*) You would be dead now. . . .

COL: You and your husband . . . would you visit my grave?

WID: He would be very jealous.

COL: We never took a picture of the three of us together.

They both laugh, start to spin faster.

COL: You had to be so light, so fast. . . . (*She laughs*) You had to have a smile so . . . so very. . . .

WID: Why are you squeezing me?

COL: Madame, the better to immobilize you! (*They both laugh.*)

WID: Are we going to keep turning around forever?

COL: Don't ask questions.

Both let out hearty laughs. They stop dancing abruptly and turn their backs to one another. The colonel creeps under a piece of furniture and disappears.

WID: What are you looking for?

COL: A knife. Or a sword. Or a spear.

WID: And I am the victim?

COL: Why, yes. (*He comes from under the piece of furniture swinging a sword.*)

WID: I ought to put on a low-cut gown.

COL: It isn't necessary. I'll get you from behind.

WID: Do I start to scream now?

COL: I don't know. I can't hear you. My ears are buzzing. (*He swings the sword over his head. The widow yells and opens her arms.*) I'm sorry your life has to end so indelicately. I would have been the happiest of all men, if I had not had to bear this cross. (*The widow howls again.*) Don't carry on like that! That's no way to do it. When you scream it freezes my blood. I'm a very sensitive person. (*She screams a third time, a high, cold sound. She falls to her knees.*) I can't wait. You know I can't wait! Bend your head down. Let me see your neck. I have to see your neck. Do you hear me? The whole building is listening to us! Quit wasting words. They're coming up the stairs. I'll have to get away across the roof. (*The widow cries.*) Now don't tell on me. Think of me in prison. Think of the men coming to torture me. Mine is the difficult role. Understand my labors. And above all, for god-sake, bow down your head!

The widow gives out a long, operatic squeal. There is a knock at the door. The colonel jumps with surprise and lets the sword fly from his hands. The widow turns on the lights.

COL: What time is it?

WID: About eight.

COL: How the time passes. (*He gives two knocks on the door. Three answer.*)

WID: We were close (*Sighs*).

COL: I'm getting a fever.

WID: We'll see a doctor.

COL: No, it's normal for this time of night. (*He gives two knocks. One answers.*) Just a minute! (*To the widow*) I would like to say something important. . . .

WID: (*Passes him a glass*) Take it.

COL: Thanks. (*He drinks a little*) I would like to know . . . I mean, it's important to know . . . which is to say, you should forgive me if sometimes things work out for me. What I mean to tell you is, I have the feeling things are going to work out for me. Well, in a round-about way.

WID: A round-about way?

COL: Yes. (*Gives one knock on the door. One answers.*) I want to know if an irregular form will be satisfactory.

WID: The first time I saw you I forgave everything. Drink.

COL: (*Drains the glass*) You can remember that first time?

WID: Yes.

COL: It seems . . . unforgettable?

WID: Yes.

COL: Nothing could ever be like that again?

The widow laughs. The colonel joins in.

COL: How was I dressed?

WID: In black. You had a flower in your lapel.

COL: Color. . . .

WID: Red. White handkerchief, shoes . . . and a yellow tie. A Panama hat. . . . (*As she describes the colonel's clothes, the door opens and a young man appears. He is dressed exactly according to her description.*) The suit was too big for you.

COL: It wasn't mine.

WID: (*Looks at the young man*) It was easy to see what your intentions were.

COL: I said something very believable. I said, "I am a friend of your late husband." (*This quote is spoken simultaneously by the young man.*)

WID: I didn't believe you.

COL: You offered me a drink, anyway. (*She offers the young man a drink.*) I turned it down. (*The young man empties the glass.*)

WID: I resigned myself to what was coming, to let the house be pillaged. I was alone.

COL: Everything was calculated.

WID: I didn't know you would also want to kill me.

COL: When you are young, you are influenced by what you read.

WID: When I knew you wanted to kill me, I closed my eyes. . . . (*She and the colonel close their eyes. The young man draws a knife.*)

COL: Unforgettable. . . .

WID: And I waited. . . .

COL: Waited, waited, waited. . . .

WID: All these years. . . .

The young man makes a leap and stabs the woman. There is a great deal of blood but no sound, no scream. The young man takes her pulse.

COL: (*Continuing as if nothing had happened.*) You screamed and it scared me. I knew I would have to act fast. You ran away from me, and . . . what sublime sport it was . . . I followed you to the bedroom. We jumped from bed to bed, from chest to dresser. . . . (*The young man stabs the widow again, then again takes her pulse.*) We screamed until we fell down . . . what fun it was! . . . we ran around the room on all fours. Not one of your hiding places could hide you. (*A third stab. The widow dies, falls across a couch so that we can see only her feet.*) . . . under the bed, inside the wardrobe, in the bathroom, hanging out the window. No matter where you went, I was there first. What a time it was! And then, when you had run yourself out, finally, all out of breath, caught between the devil and the sea, you used the only weapon you had: you talked for half an hour. Ah, but it was a bribe I was happy to take. I knew the game was over. I will not be dominated, Madam. That was your mistake . . . that . . . (*catches his breath.*)

MAN: Colonel, the lady is dead.

COL: (*Looks at him for the first time.*) Are you sure?

MAN: Yessir.

COL: (*Screaming*) Why so quickly? Why did she die so quickly?

MAN: Sir, I know my job.

COL: You shouldn't have interrupted me.

MAN: You were saying the same thing over and over. I had to get moving.

COL: But your instructions! How long was she supposed to last?

MAN: A miscalculation.

COL: I'm going to penalize you for that. Everybody tries to cheat me! (*He examines the widow, puts on the gloves the young man used.*) Are you sure?

MAN: Of what?

COL: That she's dead. How do you know she's dead? She always looked dead to me.

MAN: The pulse does not cheat, Sir. I have had a great deal of practice.

COL: Are you afraid? Do you want to run away?

MAN: No Sir. I feel safe with you here.

COL: A word of advice: Get across the border tonight.

MAN: No Sir. I have complete faith in you.

COL: Be careful. I am very treacherous. A case in point: She trusted me. There's a case in point.

MAN: Sir, you're turning pale. Should I clean it up?

COL: Why didn't you use the garrote?

MAN: It's a waste of time. They squirm. I've had some bitter experiences. I know what I'm doing. Believe me, there's nothing like a knife. Well, that's it. Goodnight.

COL: Just a minute. . . .

MAN: What?

COL: The gems.

MAN: Negotiable bonds. That's all I can accept.

COL: Help me hunt for the jewels. Did you call the police? They'll find me here with my hand in the pot. What if they do? Testify against me. And don't forget the photographs. (*Sighs with anticipation.*) With headlines, on the first page.

MAN: Ah, you have your pleasures, Sir. I wish I were like you.

COL: And what if we die on the gallows?

MAN: You have good lawyers. You're a very important man.

COL: Call the police.

MAN: The police are here.

COL: Then call for reinforcements. You have to make sure I don't have a chance.

MAN: Yes Sir. As you wish.

COL: Are they going to paddle me?

MAN: Oh, yessir. With a ruler, across the palm of your hand.

COL: Is it going to hurt?

MAN: Would you prefer to have it some other place?

COL: I think in the face. I need to be disfigured. To justify the scandal, don't you see.

MAN: May I go?

COL: Yes. Lock the door. Don't let me escape. Turn off the light. (*Lights off.*)

MAN: (*From outside.*) Anything else?

COL: Yes. How are they going to get in?

MAN: Ah, that's the surprise.

COL: Is the building surrounded?

MAN: Yes.

The colonel goes to the record player and puts on the military march.

COL: Ten . . . nine . . . eight . . . seven . . . six . . . five . . . four . . . three . . .

A window breaks. A hand appears through it holding a pistol.

VOICE: Don't move!

COL: Don't shoot! (*Raises his hands slowly*) . . . three . . . two . . . one. . . .

CURTAIN